MINDSET REALLY MATTERS

How Mindset Shifts Unlock Extraordinary Leadership

ENDORSEMENTS

Most leadership books tell you what to do; 'Mindset Really Matters' has the wisdom to focus on how to be. Dave masterfully sidesteps sterile theory by using a brilliant narrative device: two rival leadership journeys that act as both a cautionary tale and a practical roadmap. Its framework of 25 mindset shifts isn't for passive consumption: it's a call to action, making this a rare and indispensable tool for any leader more interested in genuine transformation than in simply turning a page.

Dr Cobus Pienaar, Managing Director,
The Arbinger Institute South Africa, Organisational Psychologist

In this book, Dave lifts the mirror for each Leader to reflect on how their personal mindset and life perspective shape their leadership behaviours, how that determines how their teams and peers experience them, but most critically, the impact of those mindsets and behaviours on the outcomes of relationships, on their teams and organisations.

He provides the connection between the Leader's individual style of leadership and the Leader's mindset about self and life, and how that shapes every leadership moment.

Dave then dug into his deep and vast experience in Leadership work, to provide tools on how to make mindset shifts that matter; using accessible language and concepts to help Leaders to identify, reflect, learn, shift and embed the mindset that brings the best in themselves, in others and organisations.

This book is very personal and will be a mirror for Leaders seeking to acquire, grow or strengthen the mindset that leads to positive impact across all spheres of their lives, self, home, work, organisations, communities and the broader society. A good leadership book for everyone.

Charlotte K. Mokoena. Executive Vice President,
Human Resources & Corporate Affairs, Sasol Limited

Prepare to be challenged, you have a choice in everything you do.

Reading this will help you be more conscious and deliberate with your choices as you recognise "mindset really matters".

If you are looking for a pragmatic view on how to navigate the many difficult trade-offs and choices, we must make as business professionals throughout our careers this book is invaluable.

In this book Dave provides a quick reference guide to help you think through key transitions, with real examples of how mindset translates into choices, practice, and behaviour based on real-life experience and understanding.

John Brodie, Senior Executive, MAC Consulting

First published in 2025.

ISBN: 978-1-991272-51-5 (Printed)
eISBN: 978-1-991272-52-2 (PDF eBook)

Published by KR Publishing

Tel: (011) 706-6009
E-mail: orders@knowledgekr.co.za
Website: www.kr.co.za

Typesetting, layout and design: Cia Joubert, cia@knowledgekr.co.za
Cover design: Marlene De Lorme, marlene@knowledgekr.co.za
Editing & proofreading: KR Publishing Team
Project management: Cia Joubert, cia@knowledgekr.co.za

MINDSET REALLY MATTERS

How Mindset Shifts Unlock Extraordinary Leadership

What choices will you make?

by

DAVE VAN DER MERWE

kr
publishing

2025

DEDICATION

This book is dedicated to my family, friends, colleagues, clients, and readers who have encouraged me to continue writing.

A special thank you to my wife, Esmé, and my sons, Calvin and Bradley, who have been a huge source of support during the writing of this book, my best-selling leadership book, *Your Leadership Footprint*, and my previous fiction novels.

TABLE OF CONTENTS

ABOUT THE AUTHOR

Dave J van der Merwe is a tenth-generation South African born in the Karoo, who spent most of his childhood growing up in Nelspruit.

Dave is married to Esmé and they have two sons, Calvin and Bradley.

Dave experienced a life-changing event in his mid-twenties when he broke his neck playing rugby and narrowly escaped paralysis. This has encouraged him to live passionately and maintain a positive outlook. This was also instrumental in leading him to his life purpose of making a difference in the lives of others and developing leaders who will shape our collective futures.

Dave has broad and varied interests, including writing, travel, bird watching, photography, spending time in the Kruger National Park, cooking, fly-fishing, reading, running, walking, and playing golf. Dave and Esmé also lead a Life Group for their local church, and they run a small annual charity event to support underprivileged children and orphans.

Dave is a qualified Chartered Accountant who works as a management consultant. He consults on unlocking leadership potential and impact, driving executive and organisational effectiveness, and sustainably transforming businesses through leadership. His deepest passion is facilitating high-impact leadership development experiences for senior executives.

Books by the author

Dave van der Merwe is a best-selling leadership author.

Van der Merwe, D. (2022). *Your Leadership Footprint. How will you be remembered?* Johannesburg. KR Publishing.
Dave has also self-published three fiction novels under the pen name of David Vander. These include:
Vander, D. (2018). *Shudder in the Wall: A story of deception and intrigue.* Johannesburg: Independently published.

Vander, D. (2019). *The Shudder Lingers: The intimidation and deception intensifies*. Johannesburg: Independently published.

Vander, D. (2020). *The Shudder Wars: Mastermind holds city to ransom*. Johannesburg: Independently published.

LinkedIn posts

You can follow my leadership posts on LinkedIn: www.linkedin.com/in/dave-j-van-der-merwe-leadershipeffectiveness

PROLOGUE

My purpose and passion is leadership and executive development, so talking, delivering and writing about leadership fulfils me in countless ways.

Following the success of my best-selling book, *Your Leadership Footprint*, I was encouraged to write another leadership book. While my previous book considered a broad array of leadership topics, this book focuses on mindset shifts only within the context of real business issues. Note that selected ideas, extracts, or sentences from my book *Your Leadership Footprint* have been included without necessarily acknowledging it.

I also challenged myself to see if I could innovate regarding the approach. The result is a combination of light theory, easy-to-find pointers, and reflective fiction stories, which are told using real business issues.

I have worked extensively with senior leaders in South Africa and abroad. Undoubtedly, each leader aspires to be impactful and leave an inspirational legacy. When engaging these leaders about purpose, values, mindset, and behaviours, there is always a strong dose of positivity, encouraging them to show up as leaders.

However, when it comes to mindset, something fascinating happens. Individually, they bring that positivity, but when they get into a team or organisational context, there is a dramatic shift towards negativity. I often joke with Executive Teams that they drive to the workplace with positive intentions. Yet, when they swipe their access cards, a chemical reaction occurs, bringing out negative behaviours. Whilst this brings laughter, it is also a realisation that as a group, they have made choices which contradict what they stand for as individuals.

So, what is a mindset shift choice? Simply put, it is a choice, perspective, attitude, philosophy, outlook, orientation, or words about key aspects of being a human being or a leader. It is how you view the world and the choices you make in responding to life. Hopefully, reflecting the two extremes of each mindset shift will give readers a new lens to existing challenges and create opportunities.

In the leadership development experiences I facilitate, the mindset shift exercise is a critical element in improving leadership impact and effectiveness. This exercise, along with countless examples of these mindset shifts, resulted in the concept for this book.

Awareness of shared purpose, values, mindset, and behaviours is essential to driving leadership and culture transitions, which creates exponential value. They are value-adding when they engage people's discretionary energy and value-inhibiting when they stifle energy.

Mindset is relevant in a world of increasing complexity, nuance, AI, and disruption. Add the human connection to this, and you soon realise that mindset can change individuals, teams, organisations and even nations. Importantly, mindset shifts have the potential to unlock substantial shared value for multiple stakeholders. A mindset shift requires action, making choices. Making choices in a positive direction has the potential to unlock value.

This book is about daily mindset choices we can make, regardless of context. Leadership is a privilege, the right mindset is an obligation, and unlocking human potential is a calling. Hopefully, it contributes to the development of current and future leaders. No wonder John Maxwell[1] once said, "The single biggest way to impact an organisation is to focus on leadership development."

I wish to emphasise that I have personally fallen short on many of the questions or insights over my career, including some poor choices. I do hope, though, that with experience, improved self-awareness, and wisdom, I will make better choices in the future.

Your mindset affects your energy, attitude, decisions and actions. It can fundamentally alter the course of your life.

Mindset really matters. Choose wisely.

INTRODUCTION

Mindset shifts

Mindset shifts can be overly complex when you analyse the changes to thought patterns, intentions, words, and actions. This book highlights opposing mindsets and creates an awareness of the choices you must make in each crucial leadership moment.

As you reflect on each of the mindset shifts and stories, you may want to consider these questions:

- Which mindset choices do you need to make today?
- What kind of leader would you like to be?
- What kind of leader do you want to work for?

Key mindset shifts in this book follow generic leadership development patterns of mastery, namely, personal, leadership, team, and organisation. Hence, this book explores mindset shifts or transitions for each.

The book shares thoughts about twenty-five mindset shifts. The general concept for each mindset shift chapter includes:

- A question about the mindset shift.
- Behavioural observations.
- Key message.
- Practical steps.
- Warning signals that a shift is required.
- Anecdotal business examples. These are based on actual events but have been desensitised for confidentiality.
- Reflective fiction stories use real business issues or challenges, which occur in many organisations.

Note – although the chapters follow a logical sequence, as a reader, you can start anywhere, as each mindset shift can be consumed as a stand-alone chapter.

Characters

Each mindset shift in the book is supported by a fictional story told from the two perspectives of the mindset transition. I have chosen universal characters who appear in all the stories. For the sake of simplicity, I have made the lead characters male.

- Storm is the CEO of Brash Inc. and will represent "from" in each mindset shift. The name Storm loosely means disturbance. Therefore, his character may be portrayed as negative, flawed, and at times, he comes across as a villain. This depicts one side of the mindset choice.
- Terry is the CEO of Impact Inc. and will represent "to" in each mindset shift. The name Terry means people's ruler and being gracious. Therefore, his character is generally more positive, solid, and he comes across as the perfect leader. Again, this depicts the other side of each mindset choice.
- Two other characters are similar in both stories, namely Thabo, the finance executive and Priya, the human resources executive.

Important context for reading the fiction stories

It is important to consider the context of each fiction story. Please note the next few points as a context warning for all readers of the fiction stories.

- Each story is told as an opposite side of the mindset choice.
- In the stories, some of the leadership styles, behaviours and ways of working may come across as unrelatable. This reflects the opposite extremes of each situation.
- Over time, small habits can become blind spots for a leader. These habits can become large impediments to the entire organisations.
- The lived experience of your leadership style and mindset may differ from what you think. For your subordinates and colleagues, their lived experience and perception are their reality.
- You may not resonate with the portrayal of Storm's character, but those leaders exist.
- The corporate world is strewn with leadership and corporate failures. Many started in similar ways to the stories linked to Storm and Brach Inc.

- Despite the extremes of each story, they are generally based on real leaders I have encountered in organisations. For some of these, they were genuinely unaware of the impact of their choices.
- There may be some repetition between stories (e.g. employee surveys, decision making, work rituals). This is unavoidable, as it is important to the story.

Leaders should understand the tension between the two extremes and find a balance that best fits their context or situation.

Reflections and actions for each mindset shift

Given the importance of context, reflections and actions can differ significantly. Therefore, this book does not describe the trade-offs between the two extremes of the mindset shifts. I leave this to each reader to reflect on the choices they wish to make, where their fit-for-purpose balance is, and the resulting implications.

It is important to know that there may be situations, such as an existential crisis, calling on leaders to go from one extreme to the other. Leaders need to know where their most effective leadership style falls. Hopefully, the stories allow you to contemplate your effectiveness.

Awareness of the mindset shifts is vital but knowing when to be where is even more imperative.

Closing

Wishing you success on your leadership journey.

Mindset really matters. Your mindset and attitude will determine whether you unlock your full potential. What daily choices will you make?

Mindset shifts

	Mindset shift from		Mindset shift to
	Part A: Personal		
1	Negative	➜	Positive
2	Self-doubt	➜	Self-belief
3	Self-centred	➜	Human-centred
4	Dubious principles	➜	Integrity
5	Scarcity and shrinking	➜	Abundance and growth
6	Misaligned ego and behaviours	➜	Inspirational leadership behaviours
	Part B: Leadership		
7	People are undervalued	➜	Heart for people
8	Lack of appreciation	➜	Giving recognition
9	Victim	➜	Shape and influence
10	Crisis, chaos, and firefighting	➜	Resilience and clarity
11	Disengaged and culture of fear	➜	Engagement and communication
12	Disconnected and misaligned	➜	Shared purpose and aligned
	Part C: Team		
13	Stifling talent and limiting people	➜	Nurturing talent and unlocking potential
14	Lack of clarity and disarray	➜	Framing and context
15	Stagnation & missing opportunities	➜	Open-minded, curious, and innovative
16	Favouritism and exclusion	➜	Embracing diversity and inclusion
17	Conflict and defensiveness	➜	Constructive challenge

Mindset shift from		Mindset shift to
18	Silos and wasted duplication ➡	Collaboration and seeking synergy
🏢 Part D: Organisation		
19	Cumbersome and reactive ➡	Future-focussed agility
20	Compliant, tick-the-box ➡	Focus energy on outcomes
21	Inward-focussed ➡	Customer-centric
22	Apathy and bystanders ➡	Commitment to decisions
23	Excuses and passing blame ➡	Responsible, accountable, & ownership
24	Mediocrity and complexity ➡	Excellence and simplicity
💼 Part E: Second career		
25	Holding onto success ➡	Life of significance

PART A

PERSONAL

Mindset shift 1: Negative ➜ Positive

Mindset shift 2: Self-doubt ➜ Self-belief

Mindset shift 3: Self-centred ➜ Human-centred

Mindset shift 4: Dubious principles ➜ Integrity

Mindset shift 5: Scarcity and shrinking ➜ Abundance and growth

Mindset shift 6: Misaligned ego and behaviours ➜ Inspirational leadership behaviours

MINDSET SHIFT 1

Negative → Positive

Question: Do you always have a positive outlook on life?

Key mindset transition: Shifting from negativity and discouragement to positively influencing others.

👀 Observations

	Negative	Positive
Expressions (what we hear)	• There is no hope for us. • We can't change the situation. • Things can only get worse.	• Possibility and opportunity. • Words of encouragement. • We can shape and influence what happens.
Behaviours (what we see and feel)	• Negative. • Toxic. • Discouraged.	• Positive. • Inspirational. • Motivational.
Ways of working (what we experience)	• Unrealistic objectives. • Crisis and firefighting. • Disconnected.	• Positive messages of hope. • Open-minded. • Positive influencer.

🔑 Key message

I believe the most critical starting point for a leader to be positive is to have "life balance", a fundamental building block, which was the first question in my previous book, *Your Leadership Footprint*. I describe life balance as achieving equilibrium across multiple spheres of life. When you have life balance, you are far more likely to be positive, influence from a position of strength, have greater impact, and be more significant in your personal life, organisation, and society. By implication, this means making conscious choices each day when we wake up.

Equally important is having a purpose and a desire to serve for the greater good of mankind. As a leader, you should have it in your heart to make a difference to other human beings. I often encourage leaders to bring humanity to their leadership style as it gives them significant influence. It also makes their roles as merchants of hope and positivity much easier. If you are positive and an influencer, you are more likely to be a trusted advisor to others.

Countless traits and characteristics describe a positive leader. There are a few key considerations associated with being a positive and influential leader. These could include:

- Being principled and demonstrating infallible values.
- Bringing humanity and empathy, and truly caring about others.
- Seeking human connection.
- Being resilient, bringing hope to the world, tempered in reality.
- Understanding that most things we fear seldom materialise.
- Knowing we will overcome short-term challenges.
- Surrounding yourself with positive people.
- Believing that things will always work out for the good.
- Seeing short-term challenges as learning and growth opportunities.
- Seeking new possibilities, being curious and open-minded.

Perhaps one trait to highlight is resilience, which is a deeply held belief that we will overcome whatever hurdles or challenges we may be facing. Challenges are often temporary. Frequently, these difficult moments shape us into somebody better and help us grow as human beings. We have choices in those moments of difficulty: accept them, learn from them, and move on. This certainly builds resilience, a key predictor of positive mental well-being and impact on those around you.

Martin Seligman[2] also says, "The aim of positive psychology is to catalyse a change in psychology from a preoccupation only with repairing the worst things in life to also building the best qualities in life. "I often say life is short, live it positively and passionately."

Influence depends on the aforementioned positive traits but is also shaped by the strength of your relationships with others. It also means that there is an understanding of each other's needs and what each person values. Your sphere of influence depends on whether others trust you, how they consistently experience your leadership behaviours, and how you engage others. Importantly, influence also has nothing to do with positional power. Being an influencer carries enormous responsibility and accountability; therefore, use it wisely.

👣 Practical steps

Positive and influential leadership requires action on several traits.

- Living a balanced life.
- Being a merchant of hope for others.
- Being authentic, empathetic, and inspiring.
- Asking questions, listening, and engaging.
- Actively seeking opportunities and the art of the possible.

ⓘ Warning signals that a shift is required

- Your life is far from balanced.
- You only see the negative and the downside of things.
- You approach things negatively and fearfully.
- Your behaviours are somewhat toxic and do not build others up.
- You are shunned for your negative talk and often excluded from conversations.

📖 Anecdotal business examples

Throughout my career, I have observed, reported to, or worked with leaders who are either positive, negative, or somewhere in between, and like a pendulum, never settling on anything. For the avoidance of doubt, I have also vacillated between positive and negative at different points in my career. In the experiential leadership development work I facilitate, I often say that as leaders, we are being watched 24/7 by employees, customers, and multiple stakeholders. I always choose to be positive, optimistic, and to give people hope. Once leaders realise and internalise how they set the tone for entire organisations, it creates a paradigm shift. The world has enough negativity; we need to choose positivity.

I have consulted with many organisations on leadership and culture work. Many of these organisations have become inherently negative and discouraging. Alarmingly, they have not recognised what this does to organisational health and business results. In these organisations, a common series of events unfolds. The trigger is downward business cycles (restructures) and increasingly negative sentiment across the business (disengagement). Leaders then push harder for results (cost reduction), business results deteriorate (bringing excess governance), and finally, the people impact becomes progressively negative (productivity evaporates). The reality is that people no longer bring discretionary energy to their work, and the ability to deliver falls on fewer and fewer people. This lack of positivity makes it challenging to reverse the situation.

Business issue for the two stories: Leadership impact

Reminder: *As explained in the introduction, the two stories are told as opposite extremes of the mindset transition. Leaders should understand the tension between the two extremes and find a balance that best fits their context or situation.*

Story 1: Negative

Storm was perplexed as he reflected on the downward trend in the overall profitability of Brash Inc. He sincerely believed that he and the Executive Team were doing the right things concerning the organisation. The negatively trending results left him with a hollow feeling. The visual evidence shone an unwanted light on the disconnect between the effort exerted by management and the outcomes achieved. Storm was frustrated and silently hoped for a silver bullet that would turn around Brash Inc's fortunes

Storm established a crisis committee to identify the root cause of the negative trend in results. This committee was to meet every week until they found answers. The first of these meetings focused on where Brash Inc. finds itself relative to its organisational life cycle. There was defensiveness, blame-shifting and a lack of ownership. After a long debate on how the organisation was evolving, they concluded they had a solid strategy in place, which had led to positivity and profitable margins.

They agreed that these good results had fostered some indifference, so there was an element of luck in achieving their past results. There was also a realisation that more nimble competitors were slowly taking market share. Brash Inc. had been lethargic in responding, resulting in a downward trend in profit margins. After a lengthy debate, it was agreed that it was time for a restructuring.

Priya, the human resources executive, summarised some of the discussion, reflecting on the cultural sentiment that had evolved over the corresponding period. She explained how the sentiment had started as hopeful about their solid strategy, and had driven positive energy. The period of indifference had led to pockets of apathy in the business, which was spreading to other parts of the organisation. The growing loss of market share also led to anxiety among employees. Priya cautioned, "We recognise that pushing this restructuring aggressively would create fear and cause a degree of paralysis in execution." She was met with reluctant nodding of heads from the rest of the Executive Team, but she sensed a deep negativity among them.

Storm took immediate action on the restructuring and mandated Thabo, the finance executive, to embark on a significant cost reduction initiative, which implied a headcount reduction. As these cost reduction targets were issued, executives were resistant, flagging that the targets were unrealistic. Priya felt the pressure and raised concerns about the negative impact on people. Storm was tough in his response, "Don't be so discouraging of our efforts. Besides, people will get over their negativity." Although angered by her approach, he had an uneasy feeling.

As the weeks passed, it became clear that whilst leaders pushed harder for performance, actual business results were declining even faster. Storm and Thabo responded with increasing governance and implemented daily analysis reviews to track and monitor results. This included energy-sapping variance analysis, which compounded the negative vibe in the organisation. Again, Priya raised concerns about the adverse impact on people, declining morale, and clear signs of active disengagement. A sense of despair washed over Priya, and to her, it felt like she was trying to push water uphill. As results continued to decline, Thabo was forced to make investment cuts, eliminate several corporate functions, and implement processes to curb cash outflows.

Priya knew she needed to take action, even if it meant losing her job. She finally plucked up the courage and challenged her executive colleagues, highlighting the consequences of their dogmatic restructuring. Fired up, she engaged them, "Let's just reflect on the consequences of the restructuring. We have seen organisational paralysis amongst senior leaders. Our decision-making has become agonisingly slow. We have huge staff churn. Given all the vacancies, we have an alarming lack of role clarity. We are losing our best talent and rapidly losing institutional capability. We have fewer people who have to pick up the workload. Our employees are disengaged and are only here to collect a salary while looking for another job." She gasped for air, "When will we wake up to our negative tone and the undesirable impact we are having?"

There was a stunned silence among the executives. It took several minutes before Storm softly replied, "Wow, Priya. I did not expect such a passionate reality check from you. It sounds like we needed a wake-up call. I'm sure that I speak on behalf of all of us. We need to fundamentally shift our mindset about how we as leaders positively influence others and how we show up. Let's take a short break, and then I would like your suggestions on a solution to fix our self-made mess. We need an injection of positivity. First, for ourselves, and then throughout the organisation."

Story 2: Positive

Terry felt discomfort as he reflected on Impact Inc's downward profitability trend. He knew the Executive Team was doing the right things for the organisation's sustainability. The visual evidence highlighted the disconnect between the effort exerted and outcomes achieved. Terry had a feeling that it was time to do something fundamentally different. He was uncertain about what that was, but he remained positive that the answers would come.

Terry had been invited to a networking breakfast, which had a guest speaker who consulted on leadership and culture. Although tempted to decline, he reminded himself to be open-minded to new possibilities. The well-renowned guest speaker, brimming with optimism, instilled a positive message of hope in the attendees. Terry took copious notes and had a newfound source of inspiration on what was needed at Impact Inc.

Over the next few days, Terry applied quality thinking time to the challenges faced by the organisation. After spending time on strategic thinking, he called for an open dialogue session with his Executive Team to engage with their inputs and thoughts. Terry shared his reflections on what led to the declining trend in recent years. He acknowledged that the organisation had inadvertently become negative and discouraged by external forces. He was also clear that they needed to demonstrate positivity, resilience and make changes for long-term success.

Terry's authenticity and optimism rubbed off on the Executive Team, paving the way for a robust discussion about the consequences of their actions, or rather, their ineffective action. They openly discussed the pressure of commoditised business cycles, the increasingly negative sentiment across the organisation, how they, as the executives, had pushed harder for results, how those results had not materialised, and how the impact on people had negatively impacted overall engagement levels. It gave everyone a clear sense of where they had missed a critical leadership opportunity.

Terry shared the moment of revelation in which he was shown how the leadership tone impacted employees. He added, "Some of our negativity has been detrimental to employee engagement. Their disengagement had contributed to the expectation gap in performance and results. Quite frankly, we need to change our mindsets to be more positive to engage the hearts and minds of our people, which hopefully will ensure that they bring their discretionary energy to Impact Inc". Terry looked around the room, sensing a full acceptance of what he had said. He then invited Priya, the human resources executive, to share her thoughts on how they might solve this challenge.

Priya explained how leadership and culture were strategic drivers of sustainable value. This, in turn, allowed leaders to unlock human potential and talent to drive improved performance. She outlined how Impact Inc. would work with experts to enhance the organisation's leadership capability, using culture as a key leadership lever for driving impactful behaviours and ways of working, and then empowering line managers to unlock employee talent. It was a challenging journey, with huge upside. She concluded, "This will only succeed if we as leaders are positive, show up, and set the tone at the top. Our commitment will influence our employees, and I'm confident they will bring their best selves to their work."

Terry thanked her and stated, "I am committing myself fully to being positive, encouraging others, and bringing the much needed hope our people need." The Executive Team applauded spontaneously, knowing they had found a meaningful and sustainable solution. Each executive then verbally committed to a positive leadership tone.

As Priya rolled out the leadership and culture programme, the positivity returned throughout Impact Inc., and the energy shifted daily. It soon became apparent that the programme was successful as success stories surfaced and the results showed gradual improvement. One business unit embarked on a fourteen-day positivity campaign, which soon spread to other parts of the organisation. The intention was for everyone to bring a positive attitude. If there was a negativity, they would start the fourteen days again. It continued after the fourteen days and soon became a motto for everyday choices.

After a few months, Priya shared an uplifting report on improved staff retention, healthier engagement levels, greater organisational agility, voluntary collaboration, better role clarity, and a marked reduction in absenteeism. The investment in leadership and culture has translated into a positive return on investment.

Terry ensured he continued to engage, share words of encouragement, and give recognition to each victory, no matter how small. He knew it was a long journey, but he was positive and had no doubt that the organisation's destination would put them in a better position for the future. He was upbeat as he headed home for the weekend.

MINDSET SHIFT 2

Self-doubt → Self-belief

Question: Do you have a generous dose of self-belief?

Key mindset transition: Shifting from letting others put you down to backing yourself.

👀 Observations

	Self-doubt	Self-belief
Expressions (what we hear)	• I can't do that. • I'm not sure that I can achieve that. • I don't have what it takes.	• I can do anything I set my mind to. • I believe I will succeed. • I have what it takes. I can give it a go.
Behaviours (what we see and feel)	• Critical. • Discouraging. • Fearful.	• Motivates. • Encourages. • Confident.
Ways of working (what we experience)	• Others limit or box you. • Others define who you are. • Others define what you can achieve.	• You ignite your passion. • You seek feedback. • You define your destiny.

🔑 Key message

A leader with self-belief, humility and authenticity is indeed rare and a blessing. The world is overflowing with others who will put you down, place you in a box, limit you, and define who you are, who you should become or what you should do. You owe it to yourself to believe in yourself and back yourself. The contrast between individuals or Executive Teams who display self-doubt and those who have self-belief is stark.

Self-belief is one of the most critical leadership mindset shifts you need to make. You have the freedom to make life choices. Hence, you can define who you are, what impact you will have, when you will shine, and who you will become. These are your choices, and nobody can make them for you.

I have personally encountered the projections of others in my life and career. Many have told me, "You can't. You can't. You can't." I was often told, "You can't write a book," or "You're wasting your time doing leadership development," or "You're an accountant, so you can't design leadership programmes." That may be their view. Remember that only you can decide what your limitations are. Hence, no one else can choose for you, let alone enforce this on you. I feel blessed that I have self-belief.

Others can often cause self-doubt, leading to impostor syndrome. This is a psychological pattern where individuals experience constant feelings of self-doubt or anxiety, despite their experience, capabilities, or strengths. Many individuals may not have the EQ to rise above these external views wrongfully imposed on them. Because we often seek social acceptance, we begin accepting the view of others and start believing that we are a fraud. Impostor syndrome prevents you from seeing yourself realistically. It is truly sad to see how the world and others conspire intentionally and unintentionally to deprive others of their rightful potential. I hope you're not this kind of leader.

When we have self-belief, we can positively impact those around us. As Nelson Mandela once said, "What counts in life is not the mere fact that we have lived: it is what difference we have made in the lives of others that will determine the significance of the life we lead."

Alongside self-belief are self-confidence and self-esteem. All of these relate to how we feel and what we believe about ourselves. Each human being is distinctively made for a purpose. We have unique capabilities, values, beliefs and perspectives. Having self-belief allows us to tackle the world, rise above adversity, look past short-term challenges and focus on positive, longer-term outcomes. Self-belief is trusting that your thoughts, choices and actions will lead to achieving great things.

I enjoy this quote from Bob Buford,[3] "Look for people who are receptive to what you want to do, rather than push rocks uphill the rest of your life."

You have choices. Believe in yourself and BACK YOURSELF! Through self-belief, you can make an impactful difference in many other lives.

👣 Practical steps

Self-belief requires action on several traits.

- Listen to your inner voice.
- Be aware of who you are and be realistic about your capabilities and strengths.
- Make bold decisions and take courageous steps.
- Define who you are and what you want to achieve.
- Seek people who encourage you to achieve great things.

ⓘ Warning signals that a shift is required

- Others put you down, box you, or limit you.
- Someone starts with "You can't"
- You are influenced by what others want for your life.
- You listen to and accept negative views of your life.
- You allow others to define you.

📖 Anecdotal business examples

I run a high-impact experiential leadership development programme for executives, and it intrigues me how often senior executives have self-doubt. This is frequently caused by others around them, who project their views or shortcomings onto others. These individuals allow others to define them. Most times, creating awareness of self-belief for the executive is highly impactful. When an executive is promoted, enters the business, or transitions, those who did not get the role can be outspoken and spark negative dialogue about whether the person is right for the job, creating self-doubt for the incoming executive.

On the contrary, I recently worked with an Executive Team that was already successful but believed they could achieve more, unlock more potential, and create greater shared value for stakeholders. It is important to note that this team was not arrogant; they merely had a healthy dose of self-belief. This healthy dose included bringing humanity and humility to their roles. The business results spoke for themselves.

Business issue for the two stories: Executive transitions

Reminder: As explained in the introduction, the two stories are told as opposite extremes of the mindset transition. Leaders should understand the tension between the two extremes and find a balance that best fits their context or situation.

Story 1: Self-doubt

Brash Inc. had not actively planned for succession, and with the abrupt departure of their outgoing CEO, the Board was challenged to find a suitable replacement. At that point, Brash Inc. had a poor brand image and a questionable reputation. It was no surprise that suitable candidates were in short supply. Storm was one internal candidate but was not eager to raise his hand for the CEO role.

During the interviews, the Chair enquired about his reluctance to apply for the role. Storm came into the interview filled with anxiety about whether he could step up and fill the shoes of the outgoing CEO. Storm responded that in his interactions with the previous CEO, he was often told he was not good enough to step up to be a CEO. Feedback from performance reviews pointed to substantial gaps in his leadership style, differentiating capabilities, and energy levels. He looked the Chair in the eye, "This constant negative feedback made me doubt my ability, and hence I did not see myself as a suitable candidate." The Chair thanked Storm for his honesty. This also placed doubt in his mind. He relayed this feedback to the Board, and so the search continued.

Several months passed, and it became apparent that a replacement CEO was not available externally. The Chair re-engaged Storm and offered him the role. Initially, he was reluctant, but after some debate, Storm accepted the offer and became the new CEO.

During the executive transitioning process, Storm consulted with a friend who ran an executive coaching business. Given the sceptics on the Board, his advice was that Storm needed to go into the role and over-index on his self-belief. His friend said, "You need to go in hard, cast aside self-doubt and assert yourself. That is the only way to silence the doubters." This advice seemed logical to Storm, who was nervous about his ability to step up after all the negative noise around his appointment. He also checked with his long-time golfing partner, who supported the advice.

When Storm was appointed, he adopted an assertive, tough, and somewhat autocratic leadership style. Self-doubt was always lurking, and often he would drive home, conflicted in many ways. Whenever a discussion, presentation or meeting went awkwardly, he would question himself endlessly. This sapped his energy, and it took a lot to get up each day and go to work. However, as the business performance started turning, the self-doubt slowly dissipated, and he became bolder in his leadership style.

Storm believed that the approach taken by the previous CEO was the best way to mentor and groom others. His approach was to break you down and then build you up. An approach akin to military training. Unwittingly, he started putting others down and limiting them. During the first performance review cycle he oversaw as CEO, he told his Executive Team and subordinates that their performance was not mediocre and they needed to step up significantly. The more he pursued this approach, the more he concluded that maybe his team were not good enough. The gap between his perceived view of their capability and reality widened. It started to become a self-fulfilling prophecy.

Storm occasionally sensed resistance from his Executive Team, but he kept reminding himself that they lacked self-belief. During a break at one of the Board meetings, one of the long-standing members confirmed his view that the Executive Team's performance, "It is just not at the level I would expect."

One evening over dinner with his wife, and after a few glasses of wine, she said, "You've changed, Storm. I hope this hardness doesn't jeopardise your success at Brash Inc."

Storm laughed, "Actually, it is the opposite; being overly confident is the hallmark of a great leader. It's what the business needs." Despite this confidence, Storm did not sleep well. Deep in the back of his mind, there was always a niggle about his leadership style. Much as he portrayed confidence and self-belief, if he was honest, there were many days when he felt phoney.

After a week deprived of sleep, he called his coaching friend. "I think I need to revisit my leadership approach. Whilst I am assertive, I feel that it is not true self-belief. Something needs to change." He also took the courageous step of asking for feedback from two of his executives, and did not like what he heard. His wife was probably correct; his success at Brash Inc. was in jeopardy.

Story 2: Self-belief

Impact Inc. had a well-defined succession planning process and believed in building leadership depth in preparation for any likely forced changes. Impact Inc. was successful and had an enviable brand in the market. Given the positive reputation, there was no shortage of potential executives and CEOs who would happily be considered for the CEO role. Impact Inc. preferred home-grown talent and believed executive transitions are best made internally. This was made possible through ongoing and extensive leadership capability development.

The current CEO signalled his intention to step down well ahead of his retirement. He was approached to run a global non-profit organisation, and felt it was his calling. Given the succession planning process, this did not cause any panic within the business. This triggered a well-planned procedure, designed to reduce disruption and ensure leadership continuity success.

Terry was not initially identified as a succession candidate. When the internal interview and selection process started, he was approached by one of the seasoned Board members to put his name into the hat. Over the years, the Board member had engaged with Terry and saw great leadership potential in him. When the Board member first met Terry, he was struck by his deep sense of self-worth and self-confidence. Despite this, Terry was often overlooked because he came across as a weak leader. The Board member took Terry under his wing and, through intentional mentoring, instilled a greater sense of self-belief in Terry. He also encouraged him to remain humble, authentic, and true to himself.

Terry reflected and mulled over the invitation to apply. After engaging the current CEO, respected leadership advisors, and his wife, he agreed to participate in the interview process. He realised that his strong self-belief would stand him in good stead, whilst not losing touch with his values, principles, and what he stood for. He also reflected on the uplifting feedback he had received over time during frequent performance and development discussions. Although he felt that you are never truly ready for a CEO role, he also knew that he would grow into the role.

Terry went through the interview process with understated confidence, and after several rounds of interviews and frank conversations, he was appointed the new CEO. When the announcement was made, Terry was pleasantly surprised by the widespread and genuine support he received from his colleagues, some of whom were also vying for the role. The Chair shook his hand enthusiastically and said, "Just keep believing in yourself, but never become bigger than the role or the business." Terry graciously took the counsel and made a mental note to uphold the sage advice.

Once he was appointed, Terry enlisted the services of a seasoned executive coach to help him make an effective executive transition to CEO. His brief to the coach was simple: guide me to retain self-belief, be modest in my confidence, and remain humble as a leader. The coach smiled, knowing he had the privilege of working with a rare leader, and he relished the thought of playing a small hand in his success.

Terry also reflected deeply on what got him to be CEO and the mentoring he received from others, including the Board members. He adopted *"Building others"* as one of his leadership guiding principles. This entailed ensuring that team members understood their self-worth and what they stood for. He often considered his life and how many people had talked him out of self-belief. Thankfully, he had a deeper faith, which allowed him to turn that into positive energy and guide him on his daily journey. He saw how self-belief and his belief in others unlocked the potential of those around him. Needless to say, the business results followed.

After a Board meeting, he called one of the members aside. "I just want to thank you for your encouragement and for instilling self-belief in me. It means a lot, and I can see how you played an important hand in my career."

The member smiled, "It was always there. You just had to find it and choose to use it." Terry nodded and returned the smile.

One evening over dinner with his wife, she said, "Since taking over as CEO, you have remained calm, consistent, and measured. You're an invisible CEO, yet everything is going well. Are you OK?"

Terry smiled, "Then I must be doing something right." Leaning forward, he asked, "More importantly, what are our plans for the coming long weekend?"

MINDSET SHIFT 3

Self-centred → Human-centred

Question: How do you bring humanity into your leadership style?

Key mindset transition: Shifting from self-centred and success-driven to human-centred and humble.

◎◎ Observations

	Self-centred	Human-centred
Expressions (what we hear)	• This was my success. • Keep work and personal life separate. • I only engage with colleagues at my level.	• We value human connection. • We bring humanity to work – be human. • Everyone matters.
Behaviours (what we see and feel)	• Lack of empathy. • Inability to listen to others. • Self-consumed.	• Empathy. • Compassion. • Kindness.
Ways of working (what we experience)	• Thinking you are always right. • Being distant and unapproachable. • Being dismissive of the needs of others.	• Engage everyone with equal respect. • Frequent engagement and 1-1 connection. • Being visible and approachable.

⚲ Key message

I stalwartly support humanity as a key trait of a modern leader. Bringing humanity into your leadership role requires action, so in simple terms, be human. Some leaders may disagree with this and believe that you should separate your work and personal life and not become too friendly at work.

When I think about humanity in the workplace, I remind leaders that everyone they interact with is a fellow human being, and in their own right, a parent, a sibling, a child, or a relative. No title or positional power makes you any different from the next person. Consequently, why should you be two people, one at home and another at work? This feels fake to me. We were designed for social interaction and human connection. If we can make this connection in the workplace, we can unhook people, and they will bring their discretionary energy to work. Everyone wins in this scenario. Humble leaders value human connection to unlock collective potential. Another key is basic human decency. Be intentional about saying hello, please and thank you.

There are many traits to being human-centred and bringing humanity to the workplace. For the sake of brevity, I touch on only six.

- Being human – showing empathy and compassion for others, knowing that each person is unique, and accepting them for who they are.
- Being authentic – showing your true self, the principles you stand for, the values you live by, and that you are relatable.
- Being vulnerable and humble – demonstrating humility, accepting that you made a mistake, and admitting that you do not have all the answers.
- Showing empathy and compassion - being aware of each person, acknowledging them, and showing empathy for their circumstances or challenges.
- Serving others – seeing the value of each person and being a leader who serves others for a greater good, without expecting anything in return.
- Showing gratitude – being grateful for what you have and taking the time to appreciate others. Never underestimate the power of a greeting or a simple thank you.

These traits allow you to live a rich life and lead others to experience life to the fullest. The enduring harvest produces magical fruits. Examples are love, joy, peace, patience, kindness, goodness, gentleness, and self-control. I once wrote down a quote from Seneca: "Wherever there is a human being, there is an opportunity for kindness."

On the contrary, is a leader one who is self-centred and only concerned with their needs, desires, feelings, and thoughts? They don't care about others and often see others as a means to a selfish end. This, too, is a choice.

John Maxwell said, "Self-centred leaders manipulate when they move people for personal benefit. Mature leaders motivate by moving people for mutual benefit."

👣 Practical steps

Human-centred leadership requires being human and showing life-changing traits.

- Being human.
- Being authentic.
- Being vulnerable.
- Showing empathy.
- Serving others.
- Showing gratitude.

ⓘ Warning signals that a shift is required

- You are self-consumed.
- Your success and needs come first.
- You find it difficult to put yourself in someone else's shoes.
- You are happy to exploit others for personal gain.
- You cannot recall when you last said thank you for something.

📖 Anecdotal business examples

I have been privileged and blessed to work for, alongside, and with many human-centred leaders. I am truly encouraged by how humanity in leadership is taking root. Personally, I continuously strive to improve my human-centred leadership style. Sometimes it is hard to explain what a human-centred organisation looks like, but what is unmistakable is what it feels like. When humanity is present, there is an energy, a buzz, a motivating current, passion, and a deep sense of belonging. I once consulted on a project for a services industry organisation with several business units. Part of the project included focussing on culture. With the benefit of hindsight, it was interesting to observe how self-centred versus human-centred leaders approached culture. The sense of belonging often pivoted around which leader pitched up, and the business results swung in favour of the human-centred leader.

Some of my early career was spent in the construction industry. Whilst I have many great memories of working with amazing people and great leaders on iconic projects, there were numerous encounters with self-centred leaders. I also admit that I had many failures in my career. Reflecting now, I realise how these self-centred leaders used deceitful means to satisfy their needs, meet their financial desires, and stroke their egos. Some of these self-consumed leaders knew how to turn on the charm, coerce unsuspecting individuals, bring on the *"we are family"* talk, and often display deceptive twisting of the truth. Given the amazing leadership development work I now do, I appreciate the opportunity to have observed poor leadership and learn what leadership is not.

Business issue for the two stories: Culture and a sense of belonging

Reminder: As explained in the introduction, the two stories are told as opposite extremes of the mindset transition. Leaders should understand the tensions between the two extremes and find a balance that best fits their context or situation.

Story 1: Self-centred

Storm was deep in thought as he tinkered with the formula which determined the executive incentives to be tabled to the remuneration committee. Once he was happy with the incentive numbers, he sat back to reflect on how successful he had been, and he held a strong view that without his drive, Brash Inc. could not have achieved what it had. He knew he had cut a few corners and occasionally smoothed results. However, he had a strong conviction that he did it for the benefit of Brash Inc. and that the shareholders had been well rewarded with generous dividends, including himself.

Storm also knew that as he hungered for even greater success, he had become bolder in his demands, including lucrative bonuses. Occasionally, he felt remorse for those he had exploited to generate greater financial results. However, he comforted himself that some collateral damage was needed to keep the business alive and shareholders happy. He was dismissive of mumbling from management and ignored complaints from employees over additional salary increase demands. He believed that tough calls were important.

Storm had insulated himself from the noise by forming a tight inner circle, whom he kept close and lavished with bonuses and expensive overseas travel. Nevertheless, he carefully limited information to individuals in this inner circle because he did not trust them to keep secrets. This connectedness gave Storm increasing soft power, which he now thrived on. Outside of these social events, he became progressively unapproachable.

Storm distanced himself from the day-to-day business and rapidly reduced his operational meetings and leadership visits to the operations. He increasingly felt disconnected from the people in the organisation and was only interested in driving hard performance metrics to improve business results. Storm also started influencing his finance team and got a thrill from doing creative accounting to improve business results, margins, and returns. He regretted dismissing one finance manager who refused to make financial adjustments that he had demanded. It is a small price to pay, he justified to himself.

He was yanked from his musing when he realised that Priya, his human resources executive, was standing at his desk. She fidgeted uncomfortably. "Storm, I am very concerned about our latest employee satisfaction survey results. Engagement levels are at a historic low, and the level of trust in our executive leadership is frighteningly low. We have to become more focussed on our people."

Storm looked smug. "Ok, Priya, but before we talk about that, did you enjoy the weekend at that luxury bush lodge last weekend?" Storm saw a half nod, and continued, "Don't worry, Priya, I'll make a speech at our next town hall. I think our employees fret too much. Leave it to me." Priya nodded but was unconvinced, leaving a copy of the survey results on his desk. After she had left the office, he muttered to himself, "These HR people over think their jobs." He browsed through the report but became agitated with what he was reading. He tossed the report aside, his mind drifting to his golf game on Saturday.

The planned town hall arrived sooner than Storm had expected, and he had to scratch around to find the survey report. He glanced at it and jotted down a few points for his address to the business.

Storm stood at the podium, ready for the live stream to all their offices and operations. He started with an overview of the financial results, pointing out some operational challenges. He then moved on to people matters, and stated, "I know that we have just completed an employee satisfaction survey, and there were some issues raised. I assure you that I have been working extremely hard to get Brash Inc. to where it is. I think that sometimes the hard work I put in is not understood. I know the shareholders are happy, and you should be too." He looked up from his notes but was caught off guard by the silence in the room. He glanced at Priya from human resources, who was staring strangely at him. Storm realised instantly that he had ignored the human impact. He faced the audience, "I want you to know that Priya will be studying the employee satisfaction results and taking positive actions to address this." Only one person in the audience clapped, but quickly stopped.

When the town hall ended, Storm went to his office, wondering why people were so unappreciative of his efforts. Seeking affirmation, he called Priya, "I think that went well. Don't you agree?" All he got was a muffled response. He suddenly realised that he needed drastic changes to his leadership approach. He did not know how, but he had a gut-wrenching feeling that it was urgent. He reflected again on his speech in the town hall, realising that he had made it about himself and not the organisation. He felt his chest burn, his body sending him clear messages that change was required.

Story 2: Human-centred

Terry reviewed the proposed executive incentives, tabled by Thabo and Priya from his leadership team. He felt that Impact Inc. were generous and amply rewarded the leadership team for their efforts, dedication, and delivery of solid results in a tough market. He also compared this against general staff incentives that they were paying out, and had a level of comfort that staff were fairly rewarded for a good year. His mind drifted to a recent interaction with a front-line worker who shared how difficult it was to educate his children on his meagre salary.

The following day, while Terry was on an early morning walk, he felt an inner voice talking to him about his conversation with the front-line worker. An idea formed as he completed his walk, and this energised him. When Terry got to the office, he gathered his executive committee for a brief discussion. Terry recounted his encounter with the worker and then shared, "Colleagues, one of our values is being human-centred, and we all care for our people. Therefore, I propose that we reduce our executive incentive by ten per cent and establish a fund to support the education of our front-line workers and their families." He paused, expecting some to respond negatively.

To his surprise, everyone readily agreed, and one executive added, "That is such a great idea. We should make it an annual commitment." Again, there was immediate agreement. Terry smiled and thanked them all.

Terry reflected on the crucial moment with his Executive Team and how far they had come as an organisation in creating a human-centric culture and a place of belonging. He also recalled the initial engagements with a leadership expert who had led Impact Inc. through a meaningful leadership experience when they embarked on their culture journey a few years ago. The focus had been on bringing humanity back and ensuring that all their values amplified human-centredness.

He was drawn back into the present when Priya, the human resources executive, walked in. He motioned her to a seat. "How are you doing, Priya? How is your family?"

"They are all doing well, thanks, Terry," she responded. "I have the annual employee satisfaction survey results, which have just come in. While the ratings remain high, I notice a downward trend in a few areas, especially towards leadership." She paused and passed him a copy of the report.

Terry browsed through the report, "I agree, the downward trend in leadership is concerning. Clearly, the lived experience is lagging. What do you suggest, Priya?"

She replied, "I think we should rerun the culture experiences we ran a few years ago. Although culture is part of our onboarding, and we practice it in the workplace, we may have lost focus on what culture means. As leaders, we need to show up and live our values."

Terry nodded in agreement, "I fully endorse a refresher of the culture experience. It was great fun and has made a huge difference in the organisation. Let's use the session to celebrate success, recommit our leaders to our values, and keep building an amazing place of belonging. I would also like us to share the education fund concept with our employees soon. It will certainly be a morale booster and show that we genuinely care."

"I agree. We can flesh out the details and share them at our upcoming town hall. I'll get straight to it," replied Priya. Terry sat back, with a warm feeling flowing through him, comfortable that they were doing the right thing. There was a deep sense of belonging for everyone, including himself.

Terry took to the podium as the town hall started. He looked up and asked everyone to stand, "Good morning, colleagues. Firstly, please give yourselves a round of applause. You are amazing people." Initially, a few clapped, but the tempo and participation increased until it was a full crescendo. When it quieted down, Terry continued, "Secondly, I just want to recognise that without you, our valued people, nothing in this organisation is possible." Again, there was an eruption of applause. Terry then asked several executives to share moments of recognition for human-centric behaviours and achievements. This was followed by Priya, who announced the education fund. All of which was met with excitement and pride. Terry concluded with a one-line statement, "Given your hard work, we have delivered great business results, and I am happy to share that each of us will participate in incentives this year." Again, the room erupted. After the town hall ended, employees milled around chatting and giving each other high-fives.

Terry again experienced the fulfilment of a human-centred leadership philosophy. It felt great.

MINDSET SHIFT 4

Dubious principles ➔ Integrity

Question: Do you always lead with integrity?

Key mindset transition: Shifting from dubious and debatable ethics to consistent and unquestionable integrity.

👀 Observations

	Dubious principles	Integrity
Expressions (what we hear)	• Nobody will know. • Well, I think it is subject to interpretation. • It's not material, so it should be ok.	• That does not align with my values. • I want to be comfortable when I look in the mirror. • I always ask myself if it is the right thing to do.
Behaviours (what we see and feel)	• Manipulative. • Fake. • Blames others.	• Empathy and honesty. • Authentic and principled. • Perceptive and self-aware.
Ways of working (what we experience)	• Culture of fear. • Secretive and withholds critical information. • Talks badly about people behind their backs.	• Show up as a leader. • Build trust and engage authentically. • Build others up and hold the moral high ground.

🔑 Key message

Integrity is arguably one of the most fundamental leadership traits and should be protected at all costs. I use an integrity model in my leadership work, which comprises five key elements: Feel, Think, Intent, Word, and Act. For integrity to prevail, there must be congruence across all five elements.

As a leader, the integrity model also means that you are demonstrating important behaviours. These behaviours include being empathic (Feel), perceptive (Think), deliberate (Intent), building others up (Word), and being authentic (Act). If you demonstrate these leadership behaviours, your integrity is more likely to be positively experienced by others. They would experience your behaviours as being cared for (Feel), being considered (Think), being respected (Intent), being engaged (Word), and being committed (Act).

Integrity should be consistently seen and felt through what leaders do, and should be maintained even when nobody is looking. By the way, integrity also applies to your personal life.

Integrity is valuable for you as a leader and ultimately to achieve business results. If you show up with integrity, you will build trust, engage hearts and minds, people will bring discretionary energy, outcomes are enhanced, and you will create sustainable shared value for all stakeholders.

One observation I sadly see is that as individuals get promoted, power can be abused, and there is often a temptation to relax on integrity. The reality is that integrity should be of the utmost importance in all you do, regardless of age, title, or standing. John Maxwell[4] has a powerful quote on integrity: "Power really is a test of character. In the hands of a person of integrity, it is of tremendous benefit; in the hands of a tyrant, it causes terrible destruction."

Think of a situation where you said something or did something to another person that you regret after it has happened. There was likely a breakdown in integrity in one or even two of the elements. Some advice when preparing for a critical interaction or engagement, which I learned the hard way, is to use the integrity model and plan the dialogue. It could save you many hours of fixing what could have been prevented. There is nothing worse than news headlines implying that you have dubious integrity.

👣 Practical steps

Integrity requires absolute congruency across five key elements

- How you *Feel* (what is on your heart)
- What you *Think* (what is in your head)
- Your *Intent* (how you give a message)
- What *Word* do you use (what comes out of your tongue)
- How you *Act* (what we do)

ⓘ Warning signals that a shift is required

- Things you say or do can be dubious.
- Having regret for something you said or did.
- Knowing you are not always trusted.
- Manipulating messages to suit outcomes you would prefer.
- Knowing that your moral compass is not always true.

📖 Anecdotal business examples

One of the most pervasive examples of poor integrity in business relates to performance reviews when delivery, execution, or performance was underwhelming. Giving accurate feedback is often the Achilles' heel for many leaders. They know they need to give tough feedback, but somehow it is sugar-coated. Not only is this a poor reflection of you as a leader, but it is also grossly unfair to the recipient. For an employee, honest feedback is often exactly what they need for growth and development. Lack of integrity has deprived someone else of something that ought to be valuable to them.

In my corporate career, I encountered many leaders who lacked true integrity. This did not sit well with me, and I found myself building up an unconscious defiance to them, something I only realised afterwards. As I became more aware of this, I also observed how leaders who came short on integrity seldom achieved total buy-in from people. The results they achieved were generally not sustainable. For obvious reasons, I cannot disclose specifics of these leaders, but the scenario above was prevalent in many organisations. What also became apparent was that often the best people with solid moral standards would leave the organisation. In the leadership work I do, I strongly call this out. If you lack integrity, you do an injustice to others, but more fundamentally, you let yourself down.

Business issue for the two stories: Ethics

Reminder: As explained in the introduction, the two stories are told as opposite extremes of the mindset transition. Leaders should understand the tension between the two extremes and find a balance that best fits their context or situation.

Story 1: Dubious principles

Storm was mulling over a key decision on a project that Brash Inc. was delivering, entailing a management judgement on a valuation that could significantly impact their financial results, due to be released to investors in a few weeks. Storm reviewed the details of the claim they were lodging for delays caused by the client. They were expecting to be awarded the claim. The more Storm looked at the numbers, the more he was convinced that the claim was understated. As CEO, he had the final say and was convinced he could persuade the auditors on the merits of the valuation.

Storm had decided that the valuation was understated and was now contemplating the quantum that he would table to the auditors. He also had in the back of his mind that his short-term incentive depended on the outcome of the valuation and increased handsomely above a certain threshold. Subconsciously, the incentive started to shape his thinking about the valuation. Over the next few days, he completed a value for the claim and then started articulating his rationale for the valuation. Once he had articulated it, he felt it lacked muster, so he decided it needed a little colour, even though he knew it was a grey area. Finally, he convinced himself that if the client saw the claim in their financial results release, it would force them to accept the claim.

The following day, his chief financial officer enquired about the valuation. Storm smiled, "It is sorted, Thabo. Here, let me show you." Storm turned his computer screen around and showed Thabo the quantum and the rationale for the claim valuation. He noticed that Thabo had gone silent. "What's wrong?"

Thabo shifted awkwardly, "Storm, those numbers don't feel realistic, and I'm not sure the reasoning is solid. It doesn't feel right or intuitive. I don't know if I can convince the auditors."

Storm was furious but held his composure. "Don't worry, I'll make sure I convince them." Driving home, he felt unsure and realised that he was probably pushing limits, but he had a long-standing relationship with the audit partner and thought it would work out OK. Besides, as the CEO, the auditors had to trust him.

Storm struggled to sleep that night as he reflected on past decisions that occasionally tested ethical boundaries. He realised that his judgement calls almost always paid off, and besides, he thought to himself, *nobody really knows, and nobody has challenged me before. It will be ok.* He remained restless throughout the night and woke up, realising that he had been grappling with the word integrity for a few hours. He brushed the thought aside, convinced that his integrity was good.

A few days later, Storm met with the auditors and explained the claim valuation and rationale for his valuation. He had rehearsed his story several times and was now confident with the number and the supporting justification. Storm felt comfortable that he had convinced the auditors and missed the subtly raised brow of the auditor, who responded, "To be honest, it feels high. I will have to test it with my fellow partner, who signs off on the quality of my work."

Storm felt disappointed by the response and replied, "Look, I know this business well, and I know I have the best understanding of the claim. Please make sure your fellow partner understands this." The abrasive tone in Storm's voice did not go unnoticed.

Still annoyed, Storm went to see Thabo, "I think the auditors will sign off the valuation. They want to get their quality assurance partner to sign off." He turned and headed off before Thabo could ask any questions.

Storm approached the boardroom, and just before he came around the corner, he heard the audit partner say to his colleague, "I sometimes have a nagging feeling about the CEOs integrity. This meeting is going to be interesting." Storm felt the anxiety running through his veins like a wildfire. He waited a few seconds before entering the boardroom.

The Chair started the meeting and allowed the audit partner to present the agenda. When it came to the claim valuation, the audit partner avoided eye contact with Storm and spoke directly to the Chair, "On the delay claim against their client, we are not comfortable with the valuation made by management. We have run our numbers and believe that only about sixty per cent is justified and reasonable. That leaves us in disagreement with Brash Inc. management."

Storm felt exposed and realised that this was a career-defining moment, which could destroy everyone's trust in him. He quietly said, "I think you are right. I came to that same conclusion last night. I'm happy to accept the proposed valuation." The Chair gave a surprised look before continuing the meeting. Storm made sure he was the first to leave when the meeting ended. He was seething but needed to remain calm. He knew that his biased view of integrity almost cost him his career.

Story 2: Integrity

Terry was mulling over a key decision on a project that Impact Inc. was delivering, which entailed a management judgment on a valuation that could significantly impact their financial results. The results were to be released to investors in a few weeks. Terry reviewed the details of the claim they were lodging for delays caused by the client. They were expecting to be awarded the claim. Although Terry felt that the claim was understated, he knew that the final decision was with the CEO. Notwithstanding the final decision being with him, he was aware of the scrutiny that came with making such judgment calls.

As Terry contemplated the decision around the quantum of the claim for the financial statements, he was also aware of the impact such a claim could have on the short-term incentives. He consciously decided to ignore the influence of the incentives, as he recognised the bias this caused to his thinking. He knew full well that his integrity was important, and this swayed his thinking towards the final decision. Over the next few days, he concluded the quantum of the delay claim and ensured that the explanation for the claim and judgment call was intuitive, rational and defensible.

Once Terry was comfortable with the valuation, he called his chief financial officer to explain the calculation and thinking. Once they had reviewed the numbers, Thabo commented, "This looks good, Terry; however, I have two comments. First, I think the assumption about time is slightly overstated, but not that material. Second, I think the damage caused by the delays hit us hard. We can increase the claim by at least thirty per cent."

Terry queried Thabo's thinking. Although his reasoning appeared logical, it did not resonate, nor was it rational. Terry promised to think it over. Thabo added, "I also think we deserve the incentive, given how hard we worked to recover on the project." Terry opted not to respond.

Terry was restless that evening, aware of Thabo's view and that the final decision would impact his credibility. He had worked his entire career, striving for integrity, and he was not about to change that. He decided that he would stick to his guns on this matter. The peace of mind he got from an unquestionable reputation was more important than an immediate financial reward.

Terry was due to meet alone with the auditors the following day, but on his way to work, he decided to invite Thabo. Arriving at the meeting, he sat down and took the auditors through the valuation and supporting reasoning. Once he was done, he showed that the chief financial officer had a different view. The auditors thanked Terry before responding, "We have done our independent calculation and believe it is about twenty per cent higher than what you have, Terry, but not as high as Thabo's. Given that it is your call, what do you want to do?"

Terry was quiet for a few minutes and replied, "I think we can settle on another ten per cent above what I had. Given the various data points in front of us, it would make me comfortable." The auditors nodded in agreement, made notes and ended the meeting.

After they had left the room, Thabo said, "I felt strongly about a higher number, but I have to admire the principles you stand for."

Terry smiled at the compliment and thought he would use it as a teaching moment. "You know, Thabo, it can take years to build your reputation, and minutes to destroy. Upholding your integrity is a fundamental building block in a career." Thabo nodded, grateful for the gentle reminder.

The Chair opened the audit meeting. They worked through the various agenda items until they came to the delay claim. The audit partner shared what had happened in arriving at the final quantum and showed that agreement had been reached and that the auditors would sign off on the number. The Chair nodded and thanked everyone for upholding high ethical standards. The rest of the meeting was uneventful.

As everyone was leaving, the Chair called Terry over and stated, "The audit partner told me what happened in getting to the valuation decision. We both agreed that your integrity is highly valued in this business." Terry nodded in appreciation. The Chair continued, "Oh, and the Board understands the impact on short-term incentives. Given your approach, we will apply some discretion to ensure the management team is appropriately rewarded." Terry thanked him, aware that doing the right thing always pays off.

MINDSET SHIFT 5

Scarcity and shrinking ➜ Abundance and growth

Question: Do you have an abundance and growth mindset?

Key mindset transition: Shifting from reductionist to more than enough for everyone.

👀 Observations

	Scarcity and shrinking	**Abundance and growth**
Expressions (what we hear)	• Tell and instruct. • That will never work. • Cost reduction mindset first.	• How do we create abundance? • What is the art of the possible? • Is there a growth opportunity?
Behaviours (what we see and feel)	• Limiting and rigid. • Initial response is always "No" • Defensive to new ideas.	• Open and probing questions. • Courage to try new things. • Consider bias and other views.
Ways of working (what we experience)	• Incremental changes preferred. • Maintain status quo – do the bare minimum. • Innovation is discouraged.	• Allow step-change experiments. • Do things better and try new ways or approaches. • Create an enabling environment.

🔑 Key message

Leaders who espouse an abundance and growth mindset are more likely to create exponential value than someone with a scarcity and shrinking mindset. We have all heard the adage that the glass is either half full or half empty. I like to refer to an overflowing cup versus an empty one. The reality is that most people want to be associated with a business or team where the cup is overflowing. However, it is startling to see how many organisations are staring at a cup that is rapidly emptying or is already empty and are reactive in responding or changing their mindset.

Being curious, open-minded, and having a continuous learning orientation are traits of a growth mindset, which is essential for a leader aspiring to unlock latent energy and value. Being curious, asking open-ended questions, seeing things from different lenses or perspectives, and practising intentional listening means being aware that we have limitations on how much we know. There is always a better and smarter way. Leaders with an abundance and growth mindset are more likely to connect the dots and harness the collective potential of individuals, teams, and the organisation.

An abundance mindset is about making choices with the view that there are adequate opportunities, resources, and prospects for everyone. Opportunities are not finite, similar to the overflowing cup I mentioned. It implies growth, opportunities, happiness and prosperity for everyone. It does of course require many people to make different mindset choices. With this mindset shift, what is important is striking a balance, depending on the context and reality of the situation. Oprah Winfrey once said, "When you focus on what you have, your abundance increases." I have observed that when you focus on what you don't have, the world and its opportunities shrink around you.

In many of my leadership interventions, I ask teams to visualise what it would look like if everyone is operating at full potential versus what it would look like if only some people committed themselves fully. Whilst it is aspirational to think of everyone working together to unlock the full potential of a team or an organisation, this reality is often difficult to achieve. It is also important to recognise that a team working together can achieve far more than they can individually. Sadly, organisations find themselves in a position where teams are not fulfilling their potential and are not committed. This correlates with global statistics, which show that approximately two-thirds of the worldwide workforce is disengaged.

A scarcity and shrinking mindset often focuses on value protection, incremental change, and cost reduction, which is accompanied by negative language. Conversely, an abundance and growth mindset focuses on opportunity and unlocking potential. This mindset brings positivity, clarity on the "why", engages hearts and minds, and taps into latent energy. When everyone brings discretionary energy, so much more is possible. An abundance and growth mindset opens up far greater opportunities and possibilities.

Each of us has been given talents, and at the end of life, we will account for what we did with our talents. Bob Buford[5] asks a profound question, which complements this abundance mindset, "What are you going to do with all that you've been given?"

👣 Practical steps

Inspirational leadership requires action on several traits.

- Being consistently curious.
- Lifelong learning orientation.
- Open-minded.
- Asking open-ended questions.
- Learning from mistakes.

ⓘ Warning signals that a shift is required

- You are not open to new ideas and thinking.
- You don't ask enough questions.
- You don't believe in changing what works.
- You believe cutting costs is the best way to save a business.
- Your business has reached maturity in efficiency and effectiveness.

📖 Anecdotal business examples

As industries and business offerings become commoditised, it becomes a natural consequence that the leaders adopt a survival mode approach by shrinking capital expenditure and embarking on cost reduction exercises. The sentiment becomes increasingly negative, which triggers even more cost reduction. Business results decline, and the impact on leaders and people becomes increasingly traumatic. This is not sustainable, and sadly, very pervasive. Having worked in an organisational effectiveness and business performance consulting environment, only leaders and people with a different mindset can turn things around. Although it may feel counterintuitive, it is superior in unlocking sustainable value.

Similarly, I have observed how organisations embark on cost reduction but forget to exit that cycle. Sadly, this is not an isolated occurrence. I recently engaged with a large organisation where the overemphasis on cost was paralysing innovation, business acumen, and opportunity. I challenged the leaders to change their mindset and language from cost reduction and negative connotations to profitable margin and opportunity. The organisation reversed years of declining margins.

Business issue for the two stories: Cost reduction versus profitable growth

Reminder: As explained in the introduction, the two stories are told as opposite extremes of the mindset transition. Leaders should understand the tensions between the two extremes and find a balance that best fits their context or situation.

Story 1: Scarcity and shrinking

Brash Inc. was caught in a vicious cycle of poor economic growth, inflationary pressures, and hugely negative consumer sentiment. It was arguably the toughest trading year the business had experienced in over a decade. As CEO, Storm felt the pressure and was fearful, although he was trying not to show it.

It was Monday morning, and Storm dragged himself out of bed. He had initiated a weekly morning meeting to focus on cost reduction and preserving cash flow. Much as it was his idea, he felt the energy drain from him at the thought of sitting through yet another half-day of analysis and beating the cost reduction drum. Aware that he needed to keep up the morale, he mustered all his energy and entered the conference room. The negative energy in the room seemed to leap at him, smother him, and he sat down heavily.

Even though he could recite the agenda perfectly, he reminded everyone of the key items: reduce costs, cut headcount, and conserve cash. He looked up and started the meeting, "Can everyone please give us detailed feedback on cost reduction efforts in your area?" One after the other, his Executive Team went through many PowerPoint slides, repeating the same themes that had been said for the last few months. The message remained the same. Costs had been cut to the bone. However, the tone became more morbid each week. Feedback on reducing headcount was even more dire, as the business lost good people and productivity declined. Cash flow pressures remained challenging, and it was a daily scramble to pay suppliers. He left the meeting deflated. In all his years as CEO, he had never felt so depressed.

Storm sat glumly with his weekend golf buddies. "Still having fun with your cost reduction?" one of them chirped. For Storm, it was a stale joke. Another added, "Maybe try different approaches to cost reduction instead of the blanket approach you have been using. There are different approaches, mix it up a bit." This suggestion lifted Storm's mood somewhat, and after probing a few ideas, he agreed to try something different.

For a change, Storm was energised to go to work on Monday. He skipped the agenda and suggested they brainstorm new ways to reduce costs. It was painful, but they considered strategic sourcing, supply chain optimisation, process simplification, reducing product lines, changing packaging, reducing extra services, and reducing product sizes. Storm was happy with the discussion, but the feedback was muted. It felt like more of the same.

It wasn't long before it was back to normal, with no real changes having been made and cash flow pressures continuing. This forced Storm and the team to announce another round of cost removals, headcount reduction, and budget cuts. Storm believed the worst was over and did his best to rally the Executive Team to think positively and demonstrate more resilience. The team nodded in agreement, but Storm did not get a sense of commitment. After twelve months, he was disheartened. He realised that his mindset was firmly in shrinking mode.

In desperation, he called an old friend and asked for advice. After elaborating and sharing the business context, his friend stated: "I assume you're seeing organisational paralysis, your management is negative, and your employees are disengaged." Storm dejectedly nodded at this reality. His friend sighed, "You cannot cut or shrink your way to success. You must change the lens and focus on the real value drivers: your leaders, people, and customers. You need to shift the organisational mindset from cost reduction to a profitable business. Only then will you stand a chance."

Storm slowly nodded, aware of the new reality. Inside, he was churning. How had he led the organisation to be so narrow-minded? He realised it was far from over, and there was to be more trauma before they turned anything around.

Storm consulted with a leadership expert who guided him by linking an abundance mindset with an understanding of the drivers of growth at Brash Inc. By stepping back and applying some deep strategic thinking, he was able to plot a way forward. He felt a glimmer of hope from within, comforted in the knowledge that he could articulate the building blocks to a different reality.

Story 2: Abundance and growth

Impact Inc. was caught in a difficult cycle of declining economic growth, supplier margin pressure, and negative consumer sentiment. It was arguably one of the toughest trading years the business had experienced in over a decade. Terry was aware of the pressure on the organisation but showed authenticity in acknowledging it. He also knew that his mindset could sway his team and the business.

Terry had implemented a bi-weekly business review meeting to assess the business impacts, explore new ideas, and update forecasts. Whilst it was a drain on energy and time, Terry ensured everyone understood the urgency of the situation and the review meeting. Terry remained positive but had to admit that seeking new ways to save money was challenging. He also realised how difficult it is to shift mindsets to reverse a negative trend. He continued to explain why growth was so important for future sustainability.

In facilitating the review sessions, Terry clarified he did not want endless PowerPoint slides but rather to have a conversation on a few key things to act on and then provide feedback on what worked and what did not. Even so, the business context was difficult, and ideas were incremental at best. Terry continued coaching his team to see the potential avenues to success and not accept defeat. He reminded them that a scarcity mindset had already bankrupted one of their fringe competitors.

During an externally facilitated workshop, Terry and his Executive Team were introduced to the concept of polarity, which is two opposing sides to an issue, creating conflicting tensions. Through a facilitated role play, they were challenged to consider the polarity between cost reduction and profitable margin. It dawned on Terry that they had become overly focussed on the extreme of cost reduction. Through robust discussions with his team and the facilitator, they found middle ground on the opposing tensions the business was facing. Although the polarity exercise was light-hearted, it taught each of them a hard business lesson.

After applying quality thinking time, Terry restructured the business review meeting, and for every cost reduction idea tabled, each member also had to present two growth or profit opportunities. This necessarily forced each member to think differently. It drastically shifted the focus from shrinking to abundance, growth, and improving profit margins. It felt like someone had injected an electrical charge into the organisation, and the mood among leaders changed. They did not lose sight of reality but looked at the world differently.

Terry and Thabo, the financial executive, also reassessed all metrics and key performance indicators, and hastily removed those metrics that were driving the wrong behaviours, especially those related to cost reduction. Within weeks, a positive momentum shift within the business was evident. While the laser focus on costs and cash remained, there was greater willingness to invest in revenue growth, productivity or margin improvement.

In his leadership visits, Terry emphasised that the business required a multi-pronged focus on cost, margin improvement, and profitable revenue growth. It also became apparent that several improvement opportunities were missed because of the narrow cost focus. Terry was also encouraged during these visits as he noticed new ideas surfacing. He also observed a willingness to ask open-ended questions and to debate opportunities more freely. This was tangible proof that the business was shifting towards a growth and abundance mindset.

In a reflective discussion with a trusted business advisor, Terry acknowledged he had held an overly narrow focus. With hindsight, valuable opportunities were missed. The advisor nodded and replied, "That may be true, but more important is that you have identified the narrow mindset and helped the organisation transition to a different way of looking at the business." Terry nodded, aware that the advisor was right. Impact Inc. could face the coming trading period with more confidence. Knowing that they were doing more of the right things and doing them more effectively.

Terry made a mental note to use his next quiet time to be more intentional about capturing the insights of a growth and abundance mindset. Not only would this get them through the short term, but if consistently applied, it could give them a long-term competitive advantage. By connecting the dots with a growth mindset, he opened up the possibility of unlocking greater potential from his leadership and people at Impact Inc. He sat back, excited that the organisation was on a path to a better future.

MINDSET SHIFT 6

Misaligned ego and behaviours ➜ Inspirational leadership behaviours

Question: Is your leadership style an inspiration to others?

Key mindset transition: Shifting from self-importance and a misaligned ego to self-awareness and an inspirational impact on others.

👀 Observations

	Misaligned ego and behaviours	**Inspirational leadership behaviours**
Expressions (what we hear)	• How can they behave like that? • I'm the boss, do as I tell you. • My position gives me the right to special treatment.	• Positive messages of hope. • Provides support and infuses energy. • Role models and influences positive behaviours.
Behaviours (what we see and feel)	• Individual ego comes first. • Takes personal glory. • The loudest voice dominates/wins.	• Encourages and inspires. • Fully present in the moment. • Motivate others to be better.
Ways of working (what we experience)	• Culture of fear (leader control) • Ego blinds someone to others around them. • Poor team dynamics are allowed, which become toxic.	• Behaviours and actions are congruent. • Poor behaviour is called out. • Give recognition and celebrate success.

🔑 Key message

Great leaders are acutely aware of their impact on others. Leadership is about serving and inspiring others, teams, organisations, and society.

They recognise that leadership is a privilege rather than an entitlement. Inspirational leadership starts with yourself and how you, as a leader, internalise, embrace, and live the organisational culture. This self-awareness is essential for a leader to be inspirational. They constantly seek feedback to ensure they are making the necessary adjustments to lead effectively.

An inspirational leader encourages, nudges, motivates, gives hope, and infuses energy into others. They unlock potential that you may not see for yourself. Inspirational leaders take others from dreams to a place they may not have imagined possible, to a lived reality of passion and a fulfilled life. Napoleon Bonaparte said a few centuries ago, "A leader is a dealer in hope." Or in other words, merchants of hope. This is profound, and leaders must be aware of their role in giving hope to others and showing a positive future.

From an organisational point of view, leaders need to be intentional about leadership capability and development. This leadership capability should include soft skills and behavioural aspects, essential to unlocking human potential. Without people, you can achieve very little as a leader. When you show you care about people, then significant things are possible. Hence, inspirational leadership is a strategic imperative, encompassing leadership purpose, mindset shifts, behaviours, appropriate ways of working and showing up in crucial moments.

Inspirational leadership entails intentional actions such as:

- Consistently upholding your integrity.
- Demonstrating positivity and resilience.
- Bringing humanity to the workplace.
- Showing authenticity and humility towards others.
- Actively listening to others.
- Asking powerful questions.
- Bringing hope even in difficult circumstances.
- Actively seeking to find the gold in others.
- Intentionally investing time in others to show them what is possible.
- Supporting and encouraging others to take action.
- Giving recognition and freely celebrating the success of others.
- They do all of this to make a difference to others.

Daniel Goleman[6] explains leadership behaviours in a great way, "Understanding the powerful role of emotions in the workplace sets the best leaders apart from the rest – not just in tangibles such as better business results and the retention of talent, but also in the all-important intangibles, such as higher morale, motivation and commitment."

Every day presents an opportunity to inspire others and create a lasting impact. Live life passionately.

👣 Practical steps

Inspirational leadership requires action on several personal traits.

- Living a balanced life.
- Being grounded by unshakable values.
- Leading a life of integrity.
- Being empathetic.
- Creating a positive influence.
- Caring and showing respect for others.
- Serving for the benefit of others.

ⓘ Warning signals that a shift is required

- Your leadership role is all about your ego and self-importance.
- Not caring about what others think, as long as you get what you want.
- If something goes wrong, it is someone else who is the problem.
- Not making time for self-reflection or getting feedback.

📖 Anecdotal business examples

There are many examples of leaders who have an ego that becomes bigger than the organisation. This ego is habitually accompanied by undesirable behaviours, which are often used to influence and coerce in an unhealthy way. I have seen and worked for some of these leaders. I did not see them as role models, and if I am honest, sometimes I resented them. This begs the question: What kind of leader do you want to be? One of the most public examples in modern business was Marcus Jooste, the former CEO of Steinhoff. While I will not detail the specifics, his example demonstrates how his arrogant ego became bigger than the business; he bullied and manipulated, demonstrated extreme greed, and ultimately destroyed people, livelihoods and wealth. In my view, this is certainly not inspirational.

Fortunately, I have also encountered many inspirational leaders during my career and in consulting. As a leadership development consultant, I run a high-impact Exponential Leadership Experience (E.L.E.) for executives. Our intervention always starts with executives sharing their life story. While these stories allow us to understand the executive better, they also forge a deeper connection with the individual. I have run well over a hundred individual sessions with seasoned executives, and what strikes me the most is the significant correlation between humble beginnings, a purposeful connection with humanity, gratitude for life, and inspirational leadership. Whilst this does not hold true for everyone, it highlights a desire to make a difference in the lives of others.

Business issue for the two stories: Culture of fear/psychological safety

Reminder: As explained in the introduction, the two stories are told as opposite extremes of the mindset transition. Leaders should understand the tensions between the two extremes and find a balance that best fits their context or situation.

Story 1: Misaligned ego and behaviours

Storm sat back in his leather chair, feet up on the oak desk, surveying his huge corner office. He thought, *I deserve this and more, given how hard I have driven this organisation over the years.* He reflected that without him, nothing would have been achieved; he was the driving force that had held Brash Inc. together over the years. He was proud of himself.

Storm refocussed his attention on the proposed bonuses, which were being submitted to the Board later that day. Results were not quite where they needed to be; hence, the Board had recommended a twenty per cent reduction in the overall bonus pool. Given how strongly he felt about being the real driver of the organisation, this did not sit well with him. He decided to amend the proposal to keep his bonus level. This did necessitate a cut in the bonus for the rest of the Executive Team, allowing him to meet the overall target set by the Board.

Knowing that he needed to align with his Executive Team, he proposed the bonus reductions without sharing his own, stressing that they allow the Board some leeway for discretionary allocations. Nobody said a word, but their silence spoke volumes. He had anticipated some resistance from both the executives and the Board. Should he be challenged, he would threaten to leave, and they would back off. He signed off on the proposal despite an uneasy feeling.

Storm exited his office and passed his assistant without even looking her way. He thought she was overly grumpy and made a mental note to find someone else. He did not have time for her attitude.

As he walked past the offices of some of his senior team, he noticed that they all avoided eye contact. *They are probably still annoyed about the bruising talk I gave them yesterday,* he thought. *Well, I refuse to accept their mediocrity and excuses.*

The finance executive watched as Storm walked past his office. Thabo wanted to challenge him on several topics, but Storm's micro-management irked him. Storm always clarified that nothing could be done without his direct involvement. Storm questioned every finance decision, which fundamentally eroded autonomy, leading to a stalling of key decisions. In selected cases, he made judgment calls that made no commercial sense. His finance team was low on morale, and many were disengaged.

The human capital executive held her head in her hands. Priya was reflecting on the almost toxic culture that Storm so proudly spearheaded. He had a habit of publicly criticising everyone when something was wrong and taking full credit when something went well. His behaviour exacerbated the toxic culture. She looked down at the employee survey glaring at her on the desk. Employee views of the senior team were at their lowest in twenty years. She instinctively picked up her mobile phone to look for other job opportunities.

Two operations executives sat in the small coffee pause area, opening the sandwiches they had bought from the street vendor outside. They had advocated for a small canteen area where employees could eat and engage over lunch. Storm always shot down the idea, believing that taking time out at lunch wasted working time. They looked around, unsmiling faces looking down, everyone in complete silence. One of them thought *Wow, amazing how one person's ego and strong views negatively impacted others. It is no wonder so many people are claiming mental health issues.*

A junior staffer sat solemnly at her desk. She hated the ego culture that everyone around her was desperate to emulate. If she had a choice, she would look for another job. She abhorred how her colleagues behaved, especially in recent weeks leading up to bonus time. She could not relate to how everyone tried to prove they were more important than anyone else on the team. The lack of authenticity and undue pressure were eating at their souls. She was startled when someone walked past, bumping her desk, realising she had been zoned out for over an hour. She looked at her watch, only thirty minutes before I could leave the office.

Storm reclined back in his chair at the golf club. Over lunch, he casually mentioned to his friends how tired he was of kicking butt to get anything done. One of them laughed loudly, "It is obvious," he said, "You need to set clearer expectations and spell out the consequences of non-performance."

Storm sat back and took another gulp of beer, a clear message forming in his mind. He was tired of solely driving the business and having to do all the work himself. He messaged his assistant to set up a two-hour meeting for that evening. He told her the meeting would start promptly at 6 pm so that no time would be wasted during normal working hours.

As the mandatory meeting request flashed on emails, an audible groan could be heard throughout the office. Shoulders sagged, heads dipped, and minds checked out. The mandatory meeting request landed like a weight on every desk—another reminder of what the leadership culture had become.

Story 2: Inspirational leadership behaviours

Terry sat back at his desk in an open-plan office with other executives. The Executive Team had agreed mutually to the open-plan arrangement, as it would create greater visibility and accessibility to employees. Terry felt blessed being surrounded by great colleagues. Without them and the thousands of dedicated employees, Impact Inc. would not have achieved the success it now enjoys.

Grateful for their collective efforts, he focussed on the bonus proposal, which was being submitted to the Board in a few days. He was intentional about being early and allowing ample time for engagement with his Executive Team. He reflected again on the Board's generous bonus allocation for himself. He remained resolute that he would take the same percentage as the other executives and use the balance of the bonus pool to bolster the rewards for some of Impact Inc's front-line customer employees. He was acutely aware of the positive customer experience they created. Without those front-line workers, success for the organisation would be elusive. Satisfied with the merits of his decision, he signed off on the proposal for submission.

His assistant came up and quietly placed a cappuccino on his desk. He looked up, "Thank you. I want to say that I appreciate you for always supporting me. It means a lot knowing you make my job smooth sailing." Grinning from ear to ear, she walked away.

Terry reflected again on yesterday's impactful meeting, where it was visible that this Executive Team meant business when it came to inspirational leadership, and that they were acutely aware of how their leadership behaviours were a key driver of sustainable enterprise value.

The finance executive stood at a whiteboard, brainstorming ideas to unlock value in one of the struggling business units. Terry always encouraged quality thinking time. Over the years, quality thinking has allowed him to simplify finance, streamline reporting, and shift to value-adding business partnering. Thabo glanced over at Terry, realising that their strong partnership set the tone for leadership and created a catalyst for motivating all employees to strive for better financial results.

The human capital executive felt energised after their meeting yesterday. For many years, Priya had appreciated the power of leaders in inspiring others. Terry and she had been fully aligned on how they would bring servant leadership to their leadership philosophy, and notably, how this manifested in improved business performance. She also smiled at how her mantra, "Believe in myself," had been ingrained into every tentacle of the organisation. Everywhere in Impact Inc., people were motivated and encouraged each other. She glanced at an award on the wall, "Leadership Team of the Year." The award was not a coincidence.

Two operations executives sat down at a table with employees in the dining room area. Over the years, the staff kitchen and dining room became a focal point for engaging, networking, building culture, and often the source of some of the best ideas in the business. The head of manufacturing greeted everyone and, over lunch, asked each person to share how they were doing personally. He enjoyed this, for as much as it energised all the employees, he took it as a personal energiser. As they were wrapping up, a new graduate asked for a few minutes to share an idea. "Sure, come and see me later this afternoon. I would love to hear it."

A junior staffer sat at her desk. She thrived in the inspiring culture that filled the air at Impact Inc. She was eager to bring her best self to work each day and made a daily mental note of how executives and management at all levels sought to inspire and motivate. She fed off this energy like a hungry lion, and more importantly, she could see the positive impact on her family life. She loved her work, and most days was surprised that the day flew past, as she was engrossed in doing meaningful work. As she exited the office, a recruiter called about an amazing opportunity. "No thanks. I am not interested. I work for the best already."

Terry sat back at the industry roundtable on leadership. As he shared his story of how they led the business at Impact Inc., he could see knowing looks and nodding heads. He had long since realised how powerful their leadership story was, and he was personally fulfilled that he could share his success with other captains of industry. As he wrapped up his speech, he said to the leaders present, "The destiny of our society is up to us. We are merchants of hope. Together, we can and must do it."

On his way to conducting a visible felt leadership appointment, he received a message from his assistant. "Just a heads up, everything is on track for our annual employee leadership awards evening." Terry smiled; it was an evening he always treasured.

PART B

LEADERSHIP

Mindset shift 7: People are undervalued ➜ Heart for people

Mindset shift 8: Lack of appreciation ➜ Giving recognition

Mindset shift 9: Victim ➜ Shape and influence

Mindset shift 10: Crisis, chaos, and firefighting ➜ Resilience and clarity

Mindset shift 11: Disengaged and culture of fear ➜ Engagement and communication

Mindset shift 12: Disconnected and misaligned ➜ Shared purpose and aligned

MINDSET SHIFT 7

People are undervalued → Heart for people

Question: Does your leadership style reflect an authentic heart for people?

Key mindset transition: From not valuing people to putting people at the centre of everything and bringing humanity back to the workplace.

👀 Observations

	People are undervalued	Heart for people
Expression (what we hear)	• Talking behind people's backs. • Lack of human decency (hello, please, and thank you) • Absent leadership.	• Words reflect authenticity, empathy & care. • Check in, and how are you doing? • Gratitude and saying thank you.
Behaviours (what we see and feel)	• Favouritism & people undervalued. • Ignoring and avoiding human interaction. • Demanding and unrealistic.	• Visible and approachable. • An authentic and human connection is valued. • Recognition and contribution are valued.
Ways of working (what we experience)	• Disregard work-life balance with unreasonable demands. • Avoid mental health issues. • Closed door/ hierarchical.	• People come first, no agendas. • Know team strength and passion. • Treat everyone fairly and consistently.

🔑 Key message

Great leaders bring humanity to their leadership style. They believe that because we are human beings, we should be human in our leadership roles. Leaders should know they are being watched 24/7, so what they do every moment is critical. You may not be aware, but someone, somewhere is acutely aware of how you treat people, what you say, what you do, and of course what you do not do.

Bringing humanity to your leadership style should not be superficial. It means having a genuine heart for people. Putting people first in everything you do is essential for effective leadership. There are many descriptors for leadership qualities that demonstrate a heart for people, including: care, respect, empathy, kindness, humility, compassion, authenticity, and support. Having a heart for people is not something you can fake. It must be authentic. When facilitating culture workshops, I often emphasise basic human decency, such as greeting, saying please, and thank you. These simple things can go a long way to having a heart for people.

Daniel Coyle[7] stresses that saying thank you can ignite cooperative behaviour. In his book, he says, "Thank-yous aren't only expressions of gratitude; they're crucial belonging cues that generate a contagious sense of safety, connection and motivation."

Having a heart for people adds to their general well-being, thereby reducing mental health challenges, which are fairly common.

Leadership should also recognise that holding a privileged position with a title does not change who you are relative to others around you. It is important to consider that each of us is a parent, sibling, child, or family member. When we arrive at work, being a human being does not suddenly change. By implication, as a leader, you should remain human and bring that humanity to how you engage and serve those in your sphere of influence. As the old saying goes, people may forget what you said, but people will never forget how you treated them. Your leadership title does not give you the right to be anything but human. I often ask: What kind of leader would you rather work for?

When I think of a heart for people, I consider a harvest model, which I use in pro bono leadership work in non-profit organisations or churches. Before we can reap the fruits of the harvest, we must put time and effort into several key steps, such as preparing, planting, watering, supporting, pruning, nurturing, and only then harvesting. Having a heart for people also requires leaders to develop and demonstrate certain traits, such as being purpose-led, having unshakable values, having character and integrity, being resilient, encouraging others, giving recognition, finding passion and gold in others, and finally, adopting an abundance mindset. Much of this is fundamentally a personal leadership choice throughout your life.

Practical steps

Having a heart for people means:

- Being human and bringing your humanity to the workplace.
- Connecting with people on a human level.
- Caring about others.
- Showing gratitude to others.
- Showing respect to others.

Warning signals that a shift is required

- People are tools to get things done and are often micro-managed.
- Not caring about the impact you have on people and not creating psychological safety.
- People must leave their personal matters at home.
- There is no recognition of the person as an individual.
- You think your title gives you the right to treat people badly.

Anecdotal business examples

I facilitate many leadership experiences and team effectiveness interventions. These always entail an evaluation of your team, whether direct or indirect. My anecdotal evidence is that we all have a heart for people, but sometimes we lose this as we progress in our careers or up the corporate ladder. Leaders become engrossed in their careers, business demands, or pressure for results, and subconsciously forget the very people who may have helped them get to where they are. They unintentionally see people as objects to deliver business results. They then lose emotional connection with people and make unfair demands.

This negatively impacts personal lives, including evening meetings, emails, or phone calls. It takes an awareness exercise to snap leaders back into valuing people.

The issue of mental health was pushed into the spotlight during COVID-19. Employees who deal directly with customers in high-stress situations, such as healthcare, services, articled clerks, and even retail workers, are exposed to the emotional whims and outbursts of customers. Front-line employees who deal with the customer's reactions face stress and emotional exhaustion. I have observed that this well-being issue has not received the attention it deserves. In my leadership work, I emphasise bringing humanity to the workplace, highlighting a heart for people's attitude.

> **Business issue for the two stories: Valued employees/employee experience**
>
> *Reminder: As explained in the introduction, the two stories are told as opposite extremes of the mindset transition. Leaders should understand the tensions between the two extremes and find a balance that best fits their context or situation.*

Story 1: People are undervalued

Storm felt anger rise as the newly appointed Board member challenged him on Brash Inc's approach to local communities. It certainly felt personal to him. To make matters worse, another Board member had made a snide remark during the coffee break that the organisation did not value people. While tempted to confront them, he charged out when the meeting concluded.

Storm was steadfast in believing that anyone outside their operations had nothing to do with him or Brash Inc. As CEO, his job was to generate profit and show annual growth, not pander to the annoying demands of fence-line communities. As for the other comment that the organisation did not value people, he ignored the biased comment from someone who seemed to care more about people than the bottom line or cash in the bank.

Arriving at work the following day, after a bad night's sleep, he summoned his assistant to set up meetings with two of his senior team.

The human resources executive felt her energy drain as she headed to Storm's office, expecting the normal animosity that followed each Board meeting. Without properly greeting her, Storm burst into a tirade about the Board member who had intimated that they do not value people. Storm stated, "Please tell me you concur with my views that we treat all our people well at Brash Inc."

Priya felt her heart thumping as she responded, "Well, there is some merit in what they say. We have been experiencing very high staff turnover, which is impacting productivity across the business. From the exit interviews, people do not feel valued at Brash Inc." Despite the frown on his face, she continued, "Our recruitment costs have skyrocketed, and we are struggling to bring in new talent. Interview feedback indicates that potential new hires are researching our culture and opting not to continue after we contact them." She could see the scowl on Storm's face, but added, "Quite frankly, our employee morale is at an all-time low." She might have appeared calm, but inside she was a nervous wreck.

He stood up and leaned over his huge desk, "Quite frankly, that is your job to sort out all this human resource stuff. Just make it happen. At the next Board meeting, prepare a report reflecting that we do value our people. I do not care what you do. Just ensure the report supports my view of an organisation that values people."

Struggling to find her voice, Priya objected, "I cannot be expected to generate a report that is misaligned with reality. Our data tells us that we have a people problem."

Without making eye contact, Storm sat down. "If you do not write the report, you may as well find another job. Our little chat is over." Sullenly, she got up and dragged herself out of his office. After she had left his office, he banged his fist on the table in frustration.

Returning to her desk, she felt countless pairs of eyes on her. She imagined that most people blamed her for the state of human resources, and maybe a few felt for her, knowing who their CEO was. Disheartened, she sat down, wishing she could escape to another planet.

While waiting for the corporate affairs manager, Storm glanced at the social performance report. He could not help feeling that all the excessive reporting and governance were a huge waste of time. He had strongly suggested to his manager that it was a waste of money, but Brash Inc. had to ensure they ticked the boxes, only for essential matters. There was no need to go beyond what was expected.

Before the manager was halfway into his office, Storm challenged him, "Do you agree with my minimalist approach to local communities?" The manager reluctantly nodded. "Then why do you think our Board members are challenging me personally?"

The manager shifted uncomfortably, knowing that whatever response he provided, he would be shot down and criticised. He replied, "I am not sure why the Board is challenging you, because we meet the minimum requirements." Taking a deep breath, he continued, "I think we could be more effective in our corporate social spend. We could ensure people in our local communities benefit rather than supporting a few high-profile politicians."

Storm stared hard, "I think I have heard enough. Do you realise that those politicians smooth the way for our business when the authorities interfere with us? I know that the local community will not support us. They are probably meeting now to see how to disrupt our operations again."

Storm sat back, frustrated by the events of the day. Most days, he realised. The more he thought about it, the more he grasped that his behaviour was unacceptable.

Storm sat back over the weekend, reflecting on who he was as a leader. He could sense that his leadership approach was wrong, and it dawned on him that he was overly critical of his team. He realised he had to change his mindset about people and how he treated them. It made him uncomfortable, but he knew that something had to change. And urgently.

Story 2: Heart for people

Terry welcomed a small cross-functional group of managers to a special people forum. Over the years, Impact Inc. had consistently improved its results in a people survey. One of his key leadership philosophies was having a heart for people. He fundamentally believed that if you brought humanity to how you lead, high performance and business results would take care of themselves.

Despite this ongoing success, Terry always challenged his teams not to lose focus on people. His passion rubbed off on everyone across the organisation. The human capital report reflected this positive mindset. Impact Inc. had a powerful employee brand, high employee retention, great morale, and a vibrant culture.

Priya, the human capital executive, started the forum by sharing examples of why she was proud of demonstrating a heart for people. She shared that bringing humanity to the business was a definitive competitive advantage. This started with how people were treated from the minute they interviewed with the organisation to the day they retired. Impact Inc. was highly regarded as an organisation with a heart for people. Attracting and retaining people was relatively simple.

She paused and asked others in the room to share how they felt. One indicated that having everyone on first-name terms made it personal. Someone added that it is because leadership treats each person as if they are the most special employee. Another shared how the organisation supported her family when her child underwent cancer treatment. Another appreciated that they could have dinner with their family each evening, despite a demanding shift timetable. As Terry reflected on the heart-warming stories, he knew that focussing on humanity in the workplace was the only way to go.

Those present turned their attention to possible obstacles, processes, or systems that could prevent them from putting people first. By the time the session wrapped up, several new ideas had been explored. After Priya had wrapped up, Terry thanked them for their efforts and went to each person in the room to show appreciation for what they had shared. In closing, he said to Priya, "I look forward to your next report for the Board; it will certainly be a touching summary of our extraordinary people." As they filed out, he could feel the positivity. It was clear that Impact Inc.'s approach to people ensured they brought discretionary energy to work every day.

Terry had a few minutes before his next meeting, so he intentionally walked around chatting to people he passed. Employees had become accustomed to his people-first style and freely shared news, family matters, or essential business concerns. It was clear that people mattered, and everyone knew it.

He had reviewed the social performance report before the meeting with the head of corporate affairs. There were many positives to take out of it, and he sensed they were respected for how social performance was managed within the ESG environment. He greeted the manager and asked, "I hope your son did well in his exams last week?" The manager grinned and gave a big thumbs-up.

Terry stated, "I have read your report, and it appears we are exceeding expectations on our corporate social spend. Are we doing enough?"

The manager replied, "Thank you for the feedback, but I think we can do more." Terry nodded and invited further comment. The manager continued, "My team has been using quality thinking time to contemplate whether we are doing enough, and if we are effective. We concluded that while we spent more than what was required, we could change the way we spent it and thereby have a greater impact on local communities. We have listed new ways of delivering human-centred social spending. Essentially, we advocate that all our social performance spend must have a more meaningful impact by focussing on people first, human connection, creating a sense of belonging, and improving livelihoods. This positive impact on local communities will be good for our operations." The manager paused, unsure of what the CEOs response would be.

Terry nodded slowly, "I love it, and fully support it. I want you and your team to present at the next Board meeting. It amplifies our people-first strategic pillar. Well done to you and the team." The manager smiled, shook hands, and ran to share the feedback with his team.

As Terry packed up for the day, he reflected that bringing humanity to his leadership style was deeply fulfilling and rewarding. He was looking forward to the next Board meeting, as he was always encouraged by their support when they put people first. He would sleep well tonight, as he always did.

MINDSET SHIFT 8

Lack of appreciation ➜ Giving recognition

Question: Are you giving timely recognition to show that people are valued?

Key mindset transition: Shifting from a lack of appreciation to giving recognition, which unlocks discretionary energy.

👀 Observations

	Lack of appreciation	Giving recognition
Expressions (what we hear)	• Negative criticism. • Lack of appreciation for efforts. • They are rewarded through incentives.	• Positive reinforcement. • Celebrate success. • Affirmation of positive behaviours.
Behaviours (what we see and feel)	• People are being ignored. • Effort is not recognised. • Individuals seek the glory.	• Authentic and real. • Looking for positive behaviours. • Showing gratitude.
Ways of working (what we experience)	• Unreasonable demands. • Critical of the efforts of others. • Favouritism as regards work performance.	• Recognition as a powerful motivator. • Timeous recognition. • Look for the moments when they do things right.

🔑 Key message

Giving recognition is arguably one of the simplest yet profound ways of fostering employee engagement, retention, and ultimately, encouraging discretionary energy. I intentionally focus on recognition and not reward. In my view, these can be easily confused. Recognition is being perceptive of the behaviours and efforts of others and responding to them, whereas reward is often financial and after the event.

Whilst recognition can become overly complex, simple human decency goes a long way to positive recognition. These include listening, greeting, acknowledging, affirming, celebrating, congratulating, and appreciating. Among the most powerful is simply saying hello, please and thank you. This human connection produces oxytocin hormones that promote positive feelings in the body.

Giving timely recognition is a powerful motivator of people, as it makes an immediate connection between a behaviour or action and the affirmation thereof. Motivation produces dopamine, which promotes good feelings in the body. Timely acknowledgement boosts motivation, increases the likelihood of repeat behaviour, and unlocks exceptional performance. In addition, timely recognition allows for in-the-moment feedback, which is more likely to drive sustained behaviour change. Recognition demonstrates humanity, improves self-esteem, creates a positive employee experience, and increases loyalty. It is also essential that recognition is appropriate, real, and individualised, so that it is delivered and experienced authentically. Therefore, how recognition is given is of fundamental importance. Recipients will know if it is sincere or not.

Gallup[8] conducted research that indicated that employees who receive high-quality recognition are less likely to leave their jobs. Their research indicates that employees who receive recognition are 45% less likely to change jobs and 65% less likely to be looking for another job opportunity. This reduces the cost of talent attraction and retention

In the context of this research, simple recognition or a thank you, besides being the right human thing to do, is a value-enhancing leadership imperative. Zig Ziglar once said, "You never know when a moment and a few sincere words can have an impact on life".

I also believe that the most valuable recognition is when we flag positive behaviours rather than work effort, as focussing on positive behaviour unlocks more human potential than any other factor. Giving recognition for behavioural aspects builds respect, trust, and embeds the culture. This is a catalyst for performance, productivity, and success. Generic recognition, which focuses on work effort, can lose its impact and may even reduce over time.

Looking for the moments when they are doing it right is a motivator of positive change. In the moment, engage them in why it was right or positive. This will ensure that they make a mental and emotional connection to why it was recognised and will help them understand how this contributes to collective outcomes. Giving recognition is value accretive.

Finally, in the context of hybrid work, giving recognition is important. When you do not physically see people, it is harder to see people working and doing things well. Hence, be more aware of this crucial aspect in a virtual world.

👣 Practical steps

Considerations for giving timely recognition (individual or teams):

- Make recognition and gratitude part of your values and ways of working.
- Focus on immediate or on-the-spot recognition, which reinforces the behaviour or effort.
- Seek moments to acknowledge people doing things correctly.
- Timely recognition of positive behaviours reinforces culture and makes it more likely that employees will repeat positive behaviours.
- Real-time recognition or feedback allows for coaching or corrective actions in the moment.

ⓘ Warning signals that a shift is required

- People are ignored, and leaders take credit for themselves.
- Performance discussions only focus on weaknesses or corrective feedback.
- Only negative events or mistakes draw attention from managers and become punitive.
- Levels of engagement are low.
- Absenteeism and sick leave days are higher than normal.

Anecdotal business examples

I have worked for egotistical leaders who often show a distinct lack of appreciation for others. Recognition was deemed to be the giving of a financial reward. Such ego-hungry leaders found it difficult to give authentic recognition. When things went well, they were quick to take personal credit, but when things went wrong, they were quick to be tough with feedback and even punitive in their criticism. Quite frankly, I did not value them as leaders, and in my career, I have left leaders who failed to give me recognition or show appreciation for my worth or contribution. I have therefore been more deliberate over the years in giving recognition, although I still get it wrong.

We do not often find entire organisations that get recognition right, but I come across many leaders or business units that find the recognition sweet spot. The energy in such teams is palpable, authentic and spontaneous. I also observe that the recognition is appropriate, real and individualised. It feels right and is not overbearing. I also observe a different mindset from leaders and employees overall, in that they seek to find people doing the right thing rather than the wrong thing. This gives authentic recognition a significant multiplier effect for discretionary energy throughout these teams. It is manifestly obvious that recognition is value-enhancing.

Business issue for the two stories: Recognition/discretionary energy

Reminder: As explained in the introduction, the two stories are told as opposite extremes of the mindset transition. Leaders should understand the tensions between the two extremes and find a balance that best fits their context or situation.

Story 1: Lack of appreciation

Storm was daydreaming when he was interrupted by a WhatsApp message from one of his Executive Team concerning a negative publicity article. Storm dropped into his plush chair and searched for the news headline. He found the article and read it. *"Brash Inc. is at the centre of a major scandal regarding a product failure, which has created major safety risks and has already accounted for several customers being critically injured."* Storm was ashen and felt his fury rise as he read the remainder of the article. He vaguely recalled some issues with a product a while back, but this article caught him by surprise.

Storm liked to be on the front foot and jumped into action, calling an emergency meeting with key managers from the relevant business unit. Once the team was seated in the boardroom, he walked around the desk and placed a copy of the article in front of each manager. With a raised voice, he started, "This is a scandal that I find hard to swallow. My reputation as CEO is at stake. Quite frankly, this team of managers is responsible for this disaster." He paused for effect, " I want answers and a plan to rectify this situation within forty-eight hours." With anger swirling inside, he waved them to the door.

When Storm reconvened the team two days later, he had calmed down, realising that the article had been somewhat misguided, that the injuries were not critical, and were potentially self-inflicted. He listened intently to the corrective actions taken by the team and the planned preventative measures. After the team had presented their action plan, they sat back expectant of a positive response. Storm gruffly responded, "Just to be clear, let's not make the same mistake again." Without waiting for a response, he left the room. The mood in the room was sombre, and without a word being said, you could sense the disengagement and negative energy.

Storm called in his communications manager and gave them a brief draft, which read, "As CEO of Brash Inc., I have taken personal steps to ensure that the recent minor product failures will not happen again. We also place on record that the injuries mentioned in the media were minor and self-inflicted. Even so, I am working on corrective actions to ensure that the use of our products is safe." Storm could see that the manager wanted to make his normal irritating changes, so he shut the discussion down, "Just do as I tell you."

It took several weeks for the management team from the business unit to complete all the corrective actions and preventative measures. Storm was frustrated by the slow response and did not attempt to hide his frustration in feedback sessions. Once the organisation was ready to respond to customers on the product failure, Storm closed off one meeting: "I hope each of you has learned from this mess and will never repeat it." Storm sensed their animosity but shrugged it off. Tough times called for tough love, he thought. Finally, he added, "I also want to know who is most responsible for this mess. I must demonstrate to the public that we have robust consequence management processes." His final comment sucked the last molecule of energy out of the room.

Storm issued a second statement to customers that he had taken ownership of the scandal, and that all actions and measures were in place to prevent a future product failure. "As CEO, I have ensured that we fixed the issue," the statement concluded.

One of his executives, who oversaw the business unit, asked Storm if he could host a small function to give the team recognition for rectifying the product failure and rebuilding customer trust. Storm scoffed at the idea, "That's crazy. They should never have made a mistake in the first place. We certainly don't want to create a precedent for poor performance." The executive left his office dejected and frustrated.

Storm looked around to find Thabo, the financial executive, staring at him. He said, "Hey Storm. I feel that was uncalled for. It took the whole organisation to turn around the scandal, regardless of how it happened. I also disagree with you trying to find a scapegoat."

"Are you serious?" shouted Storm.

Thabo did not back off, "I think you are out of line. I am going to sign off the function. I believe that showing some appreciation is the least we can do." Thabo did not wait for a response and walked off.

Storm wanted to respond, but words evaded him. The tough response from Thabo had hit home. He realised he had overstepped the mark on many fronts. It was time to engage with his coach again.

Story 2: Giving recognition

Terry was mulling over a strategic initiative report when he was interrupted by a WhatsApp message from one of his Executive Team concerning a negative publicity article. Terry switched his attention to the article and read it. *"Impact Inc. is at the centre of a major scandal regarding a product failure which has created major safety risks and has already accounted for several customers being critically injured."* Terry was shaken, aware of a recent product issue, but the article surprised him.

Terry was generally proactive but knew that it was important to gather the facts before jumping to conclusions and taking misguided action. He called and had one-to-one engagements with the responsible executives and managers. When Terry felt equipped with context, he called for a meeting. Once they were all seated, he started, "Firstly, I recognise how hard all of you work, so this scandal must come as a shock to you all. Notwithstanding, we have a situation, and we all need to pull together to resolve the issue." He looked around the room, sensing the pride each of them took in their work. He concluded, "With all your experience, I know you can resolve this. You have my full support."

When they reconvened two days later, it was apparent that the team had gone beyond the call of duty, taken many corrective actions and implemented preventative measures. Terry listened attentively, and once the business unit management team had finished, he replied, "Well done, guys. I know that this has taken a massive commitment from many people. Please communicate to everyone on a job well done so far." The team acknowledged the recognition with a deep sense of pride. Terry added, "Once we complete all the actions and measures, I'd like to do two things: one, give the team recognition, and two, have a lessons learned discussion to avoid anything like this in the future. Good luck with closing out the remaining actions."

Terry left the meeting feeling positive that they had accepted that the scandal had strengthened the organisation. He called his communication manager and agreed on a series of calls with key customers, and particularly customers impacted by the product failure. His message was clear: we need to be authentic in our response, take responsibility and ensure that customers have a positive experience despite the incidents.

Terry was pleasantly surprised when the responsible executive and manager came to see him, indicating that all corrective actions had been taken and the preventative measures implemented. Terry thanked the team and said, "Well done, that was done in record time. Please send appreciation to everyone involved. However, I am curious, how did we get it done so quickly?"

The manager smiled, "Everyone knows you appreciate their work, and that you gave your full support. Knowing they are appreciated ensured they brought their discretionary energy and rallied as a team. And of course, they did not want to disappoint each other." He paused and added, "With everyone showing real gratitude for efforts, it has also made people realise that their contribution matters. This is driving even greater collaboration and synergy. Everyone wins."

Terry beamed, "Wow. All I can say is that I am proud to be with Impact Inc."

The executive asked, "Terry, given the effort that went in, can I organise a small function to say thanks?"

Terry pretended to be surprised, "Absolutely not. I think this calls for a special dinner, and of course, I would like the team to be honoured at our next town hall. They deserve to be given credit in front of the whole organisation." The executive's shock was quickly replaced with a huge grin. Terry concluded, "Our people are valuable and deserve recognition when they do great work."

Priya, the human resources executive, had overheard the conversation, "Nice touch, Terry. I've been thinking about implementing a recognition programme that focuses on *in-the-moment* recognition, which focuses on finding people doing the right things. The intent is for real-time recognition for either positive behaviours or good work. This should be visible and amplify our culture. What do you think?"

Terry did not hesitate, "You have my full support. Make it happen. We can also be more intentional about calling our key moments in our visible felt leadership visits."

Priya nodded, "It will also contribute significantly to staff retention."

MINDSET SHIFT 9

Victim → Shape and influence

Question: Does your leadership style shape and influence people positively in response to an external action?

Key mindset transition: From being a victim to controlling your response, shaping and influencing the outcome.

👀 Observations

	Victim	Shape and influence
Expressions (what we hear)	• Incongruence and inconsistency in how people show up. • Victim mentality. • Trust deficit.	• Positive thoughts on controlling destiny. • Positive energy and language. • Straight talk and influence from a position of strength.
Behaviours (what we see and feel)	• Protect your turf and defensive. • Disengagement and conflict. • Passive-aggressive behaviours.	• Integrity in all interactions. • Positive thinking to shape the future. • Encourage and influence them to seek new possibilities.
Ways of working (what we experience)	• Each one for themselves. • Reluctance to take responsibility or accountability. • Poor collaboration and frequent conflict.	• Consistent engagement behaviours. • Establish a common understanding of the goal. • Build trust through the predictable experience of how leaders show up.

🔑 Key message

The role of a leader is to build trust, which ultimately shapes and influences the future. I have a model for building trust with four key elements:

- Shared purpose for the team.
- Consistent leadership behaviours.
- Agreed ways of working.
- Predictable experience of each other when we work or engage.

Using these elements builds trust, making it significantly easier for a leader to shape and influence what happens in an organisation. Following this, leaders should demonstrate certain traits such as authenticity, asking open-ended questions, active listening, showing empathy, being curious, generating ideas and applying strategic thinking.

Shaping and influencing are more about behaviour and mindset than positional power. Shaping and influencing is about the strength of relationships, understanding needs and having clarity of expectations. This means that leaders must consider all perspectives and find win-win solutions and outcomes. Such leaders can shift people and organisations from being victims to a place where they can control or influence a situation.

Some of the defining traits of a shaper and influencer from my book *Your Leadership Footprint* include:

- Be an authentic leader who is trusted, and who speaks to your character
- In all your interactions, you need to demonstrate integrity and fairness
- Your answers must demonstrate that you have considered the impact on the collective good
- You use powerful questions to unhook others (see later in the book)
- You demonstrate that you have applied your mind
- You encourage systemic thinking, which demonstrates impact and understanding of unintentional consequences
- You learn from the past and apply it to the current
- You see, the big picture can show others new possibilities
- You know when to use other influencers to drive positive change

Great leaders can take difficult situations and shape and influence people to drive an outcome that is beneficial for the greater good. This also implies a self-belief that the disruptive event is temporary and that they rise above the situation to see what is possible, and they plot the way there for others to follow.

As Stephen R. Covey[9] says, "Win-win is a frame of mind and heart that constantly seeks mutual benefit in all human interactions." Being able to shape and influence is exciting, but it also brings enormous responsibility and accountability.

Practical steps

Selected practical steps as a shaper and influencer

- Articulate your intent as a shaper and influencer and the desired outcome.
- Define the behaviours and ways of working that are required from you to enable you to lead the change.
- Craft the message and narrative relative to what you want to influence, so that you can lead people to the destination.
- Identify the key milestones for people to mobilise and enable action.
- Provide ongoing support, steer and lead from the front to ensure that the mindset shift happens.

Warning signals that a shift is required

- If something negative happens, people adopt a victim mentality.
- People focus on the negatives only, and nothing gets done.
- There is a lot of defensiveness and protection of silos.
- There are many excuses and blame for not getting things done.
- Anxiety is prevalent, resilience drops and mental health issues creep in.

Anecdotal business examples

A colleague and I consulted for an organisation that was the target of a corporate takeover. When we engaged the team, it was evident that there was a great deal of anxiety and levels of resilience were low. Whilst the initial request was focussed on building resilience, it soon became apparent that the organisation was in a powerful position, despite the belief that they were victims. We worked with the team to shift their mindset from victim to *Shaper and Influencer*. Once they changed their mindsets, we enabled them to articulate the value they brought to the corporate deal, strengths that could be leveraged, their leadership capabilities and what they needed from the acquirer. It resulted in a shift from victim to powerful shaper and influencer of the actual corporate transaction.

I have been involved in several comprehensive leadership and culture programmes, which are a powerful reminder of how leaders and their behaviours are either positive value multipliers or negative value destroyers. Integral to this is how leaders show up, live their values, and behave. Done correctly, leadership influence can be one of the most powerful value creation concepts. Successful leadership and culture programmes also require consistency and that it is embedded across all leadership levels. The positive energy and momentum that is gained is often unparalleled. As a leader, you can shape and influence, and provided you use it wisely, you can quite literally create magic. I have seen this magic unfold a few times, and the impact continues to leave me in awe.

Business issue for the two stories: M&A target

Reminder: As explained in the introduction, the two stories are told as opposite extremes of the mindset transition. Leaders should understand the tensions between the two extremes and find a balance that best fits their context or situation.

Story 1: Victim

Analysts had for some time advocated that Brash Inc. was a takeover target, emphasised again in an article written by a junior analyst. Storm scoffed at the idea. As CEO, he believed his organisation should remain independent, despite contrarian views. His mind drifted to his golf game that afternoon.

Over the next few weeks, the talk in the industry grew louder. Storm did not trust anyone outside of a few people on his team, who he knew would always accept his viewpoints, regardless of how biassed they may be. It was good to have some "yes" men on his side. The Chair notified him that the Board wanted a briefing on the potential takeover by other industry players.

He had called together his Executive Team at a luxury bush lodge. He felt that if they were to discuss such a serious topic, they might as well be comfortable. Although the agenda for the two days had been set, Storm spontaneously decided to have a relaxed first day and an extended lunch over a few drinks. He secretly wanted to distract them, so when it came to the difficult discussion of the takeover, they would be less likely to ask difficult questions.

After breakfast the following day, he started with the executive meeting, "Welcome everyone. I would like us to spend the next few hours discussing the potential of a merger and how we will protect ourselves. You have all heard the rumours circling in the press. I strongly believe that there is a great deal of fake news floating around and that we are being targeted unfairly. We are clearly the victims here. Our job today is to discuss how we make Brash Inc. unattractive and protect our hard-earned independence." He made deliberate eye contact with each of them and stated loudly, "We are special, and we should dictate our destiny. Before we lay out our battle plans, are there any comments?"

The sales director cautiously raised his hand, "Storm, don't you think that by joining forces with a bigger player with greater distribution networks, we could put the brakes on our declining sales volumes?"

Storm could feel his blood rise, but tried to remain calm on the outside, "I thought we discussed that over lunch yesterday. You agreed with me that this is just a temporary decline, and our volumes should ratchet up in the second half of the year."

Before Storm could continue, Thabo, the finance executive, raised his hand, "I think we should not lose sight of the fact that our balance sheet is strained, and our ability to settle a debt obligation at financial year-end is under pressure. A merger could provide a timely capital injection."

Storm jumped in before he could continue, "I doubt the banks will do anything about it. I have contacts, and I will find more capital, if required. I believe we are financially sound. I suggest we all stop this negative talk and self-doubt and move to discuss defensive strategies." He looked around the room, sensing that very few were convinced, but buoyed by the knowledge that very few would openly go against him. As CEO, he felt he knew best; they just had to trust him.

They spent the rest of the day discussing tactical steps to confuse potential suitors in the market. Storm brimmed with confidence, but those in the room were nowhere near as confident as their boss. When a few of them gathered outside for coffee during a break, the consensus was that some suggestions may be crossing ethical boundaries. Despite their concerns, nobody wanted to be a victim of Storm's wrath by challenging what was on the table.

Following the luxury breakaway, Storm single-handedly took on his crusade to defend Brash Inc., ensuring that the market was clear they were not for sale, and that any attempt at a merger would be met with fierce resistance. When an analyst cornered him about the merits of a merger offer from a competitor, he scoffed at the idea, stating that if there were to be any merger, they would take the lead and dictate terms.

Storm arrived at the convened Board meeting and was surprised to find all members seated and already in deep discussion. The Chair motioned for him to take a seat. "Storm, just to advise, we have just received a hostile bid by a competitor, and as a Board, we have less than two days to decide. Our largest shareholders have also advised us they support this corporate transaction. They believe our poor results and non-performance cannot be turned around without a strong suitor." Storm rose to object, but the Chair ignored him, "There is also a fundamental condition which brings a premium to the hostile bid." Storm apprehensively leant forward. The Chair stared intently at him, "That condition is you stepping down as CEO."

As Storm slumped in his chair, another Board member stated, "We agree with their condition."

Story 2: Shape and influence

Terry had been reflecting on the likelihood of a potential merger or takeover of Impact Inc. by a larger competitor. Despite the organisation's success, the quest for growth required capital, which, as a small industry player, they did not have. Analysts had been advocating for consolidation to protect the industry and long-term sustainability. Much as it pained him, he realised it was inevitable and would ensure the continued employment of two thousand employees and provide stability for the families who depended on them.

Terry had discussed the possible scenarios with the Chair, who held similar views, and they agreed to meet with the Board in a few weeks to discuss a strategy. Terry had been mulling over how to engage constructively with his team. He sensed that recent market conditions and the rumours of a takeover had taken their toll on his team, and he could see the dip in their energy.

Fortuitously, he was having coffee with a business acquaintance who referred him to a management consultant who specialised in the merger and acquisition field. Terry agreed to meet with the consultant. There was immediate chemistry between them. They arranged a workshop with the Impact Inc. Executive Team to discuss strategic responses to the corporate transaction. Terry was determined to be open-minded about a different approach.

A week later, Terry and his Executive Team met with the consultant at a small but functional conference facility close to their offices. The facilitated conversation was structured around defining a shared purpose for the team and identifying which mindset transitions were required in anticipation of a corporate transaction. The team were energised when they established a shared purpose that would see any transaction drive growth for the business and its people. The Executive Team were also hugely energised when they agreed to shift their mindset from being a target or victim to a shaper and influencer of the transaction. This allowed them to focus their energy on finding synergies, identifying value opportunities and agreeing on what they would need from an acquirer to boost their business. This included capabilities and access to funding.

Terry reflected at the end of the workshop and realised that this alternative approach was a blessing. A corporate transaction was not to be feared, but was an opportunity to change the game. He drove home that evening, at peace with a day well spent.

Terry and his team had a few more planning sessions with the consultant over the next week, and by the time the meeting with the Board arrived, there was a positive vibe and a clear way forward. He had called the Chair to brief him on the strategic thinking and considerations his team had prepared.

Terry arrived at the convened Board discussion and was welcomed by all the members. When everyone was seated, the Chair welcomed them and mentioned that within the last few hours, they had received two separate indicative offers, one somewhat hostile and the other leaning more towards a friendly merger. He said, "Before we start, I would like Terry to give us his CEO perspective on how Impact Inc. have considered the options in the event of a corporate transaction."

Terry stood up, moved to a screen, and took the Board through a handful of slides, which succinctly outlined thinking and options. He concluded, "For us as an Executive Team, the most important issue is protecting the livelihoods of our employees. We must bring humanity to our approach, regardless of the deal mechanics. We believe we are in a powerful position to shape and influence any transaction proposed."

The Chair thanked him and then handed over to the head of the investment committee. She outlined the details of the two indicative offers, giving an insightful analysis of the pros and cons of each. Once they had reviewed all the facts, it dawned on the members that the most suitable offer was the one that was perceived as hostile. After a thorough debate, they aligned around the shape and influence approach, laying out a clear strategy for approaching the entity and recommending a merger which would provide a win-win outcome for all parties concerned.

A few days later, the Chair called Terry, "I have positive news, the acquirer has agreed to meet to discuss a mutually beneficial merger, but they do want control. At least it will be a win-win dialogue rather than a hostile takeover. They also have one non-negotiable condition."

The Chair paused, making Terry feel anxious. "The condition is that you remain as CEO. Well done to you and your team."

MINDSET SHIFT 10

Crisis, chaos, and firefighting → Resilience and clarity

Question: Are you a resilient and calm leader?

Key mindset transition: Articulating the key building blocks that move beyond a crisis

👀 Observations

	Crisis, chaos, and firefighting	Resilience and clarity
Expressions (what we hear)	• Crisis and fire-fighting words prevail. • We don't know what to do. • Shouting and blaming.	• Empathy from leaders. • Encouragement and hope. • Truth, reliability and reality.
Behaviours (what we see and feel)	• High levels of fear & anxiety. • Outbursts of emotions. • Focus on urgent rather than important.	• Maintain composure. • Self-control and self-awareness. • Manage their emotions and actively listen.
Ways of working (what we experience)	• No clarity of action in a crisis. • Unable to make decisions. • Reactivity and inability to think.	• Decisions with imperfect data. • Seek opportunities to leverage the crisis. • Required actions clearly communicated.

🔑 Key message

Resilience and clarity are essential if an organisation is in crisis or has to deal with a major event impacting the business. Resilience is the knowledge that you will move past the crisis, and clarity is the ability to calmly convey the context and articulate the key steps that will move you to the future. This combination of resilience and clarity means that leaders can not only navigate the crisis but also take the organisation to a stronger, better and more adaptable place. It is imperative that leaders identify the crisis early but also take decisive actions that dislodge the organisation from a state of crisis or paralysis.

During these moments of crisis or challenging events, leaders must quickly discern the context and make sense of what is happening. This is important because in moments of crisis, people become negative and anxiety levels rise. Leaders must understand the reality, consider the future, take decisive actions and shift the organisation to a realistic hope of an outcome. This implies showing the organisation optimism, based on articulating the building blocks to take the organisation to a different end state. Leaders who are courageous during such times can often see their organisations thrive after the setbacks created by the crisis.

Resilience and clarity require leaders to be emotionally self-aware during these moments of crisis. I also believe that empathy and showing a human touch during these difficult times will create enduring outcomes. On the contrary, creating panic by ignoring the human element almost always makes the crisis more complex and drags out its impact. Martin Seligman refers to the 3Ps, which can help individuals build resilience. They are personal, pervasive and permanent. Asking yourself three questions when faced with a crisis can build resilience. Is it personal? Is it pervasive? Is it permanent? On an individual basis, I often say, *Your success rate of getting through bad days is 100% up to now.*

Decision-making during a crisis is of paramount importance. Whilst I often say, *"Never make a long-term decision in a short-term crisis"*, decisions must be made which move the organisation out of potential paralysis. However, when making these decisions, stress test them as no-regret decisions. This implies that regardless of your decision, it should not leave you with any regrets, be they positive or negative. Again, leaders need emotional or situational awareness of what is happening around them. Moving forward requires a level head.

Resilience does not imply that we try to avoid the issue or disruption. The goal is to transition effectively, timeously, and constructively through the event.

👣 Practical steps

- Reflect on your leadership resilience in a crisis and how you responded.
- Reflect on how you led in the crisis and whether you were calm.
- Assess what failed that caused the crisis.
- Consider possible crises and business impact, and assess the impact of scenarios.
- Develop a response plan, considering resilience, create clarity and key building blocks.

ⓘ Warning signals that a shift is required

- Leaders are paralysed in a crisis.
- Negativity abounds in a crisis.
- Everyone seems to be firefighting.
- Critical actions are not taken.

📖 Anecdotal business examples

I once co-facilitated a workshop for a group of CEOs from a large multinational organisation. Throughout the morning, the executives used the words crisis and firefighting. When challenged, they were defensive and somewhat aggressive in their response. I questioned whether they were operating at the right level. Several hours later, they realised they were creating the firefighting and fuelling the fire through their actions and language. They ended the workshop unanimously agreeing to take responsibility and accountability for changing their collective behaviours and ways of working. They were only partially amused by my reflection that they were moving from professional firefighters to business value creators.

Another frequent example I observe is where some leaders believe that constant pressure and stress cause positive action and performance. I have even observed certain leaders infusing crisis into the organisation, supposedly to get improved results. Whilst pressure can work in selected cases, it is not a sustainable solution for performance or long-term results. I have also observed that resilient leaders who show courage will achieve far greater outcomes. They do this by being clear on the objectives, listening, leading the change, clarifying expectations, testing for understanding, supporting, providing feedback, delegating responsibility, holding people accountable, following up and giving recognition when things are done well. This resilience also implies doing what is necessary and following all the required steps for improved execution. Skipping steps, because it may seem obvious, often leads to a crisis and firefighting.

"A resilient leader must empathise with the team during the crisis, acknowledge the critical issues, but also provide unwavering clarity on what must be done to move beyond the crisis, coupled with consistent support and understanding."[10]

Business issue for the two stories: Business disruption (although a hurricane is used, it could also be a pandemic, war or other weather event)

Reminder: As explained in the introduction, the two stories are told as opposite extremes of the mindset transition. Leaders should understand the tensions between the two extremes and find a balance that best fits their context or situation.

Story 1: Crisis, chaos, and firefighting

News channels all over the planet buzzed as one of the most severe global hurricane systems gripped the world from east to west. Aeroplanes were being grounded, schools and offices were closed, shipping was stopped, and global trade was being disrupted.

Storm was gloomily staring at the news channels, believing it was all overstated and would blow over within a day or so. He swirled the ice in his glass and flipped to the sports channels. Over the next hour or so, he received various texts of concern from his executives at Brash Inc. His response was the same: relax, enjoy the weekend, and we can sort it out next week. Shaking his head, he thought about his team and decided they were being overly dramatic. He powered off his mobile, determined to enjoy his weekend.

The hurricane system continued unabated over the weekend and only began subsiding on Tuesday. Nationally, many of Brash Inc's operations were caught in the middle of one of the localised hurricanes, and almost all the operations had been impacted by flooding, building damage, disrupted supply chains, and employees unable to get to work.

Storm was furious about the calls from senior leaders requesting a plan of action. He prepared an email on Wednesday, demanding that his executives and senior management meet at corporate headquarters on Friday. Solemnly, the leadership group ambled into the conference room. Silence descended in the room when Storm barged in, taking up his seat at the head of the oval-shaped table. He held up a pile of reports and waved them menacingly at the group. "I would like to know what happened to our production, sales and numbers last week? How were we impacted?"

Without exception, each person in the room avoided eye contact and shuffled reports in front of them. Each of them had asked that their teams work through the night to prepare lengthy reports in case the CEO might ask them a question. He called on individuals for responses, and each attempted to give an update. After twenty minutes, he slammed his fist onto the table, "All I am hearing is excuses, reactive suggestions, clear neglect of duties, no action and blaming everybody under the sun. I want results, not excuses. Furthermore, poor management has caused Brash Inc's share price to tank by thirty per cent this week. Our share options are losing money as we speak." He sat down, exasperated, "I am giving you until this afternoon to come up with urgent actions we can take over the weekend to fix this crisis and stop the chaos."

Storm felt the pressure and headed to his favourite steak house, hoping that a good steak and a glass of wine would ease his anxiety and take his mind off the firefighting back in Brash Inc's corporate office. He arrived only to find the restaurant closed with a sign on the door indicating that it would be closed for another week due to storm damage. Irritated, he returned to his car and found a fast-food outlet, knowing that he hated their food.

When everyone had settled back into the conference room, his operations executive stood up. Storm disliked him but realised that he had tremendous support, and while he hated to admit it, the guy did get things done. The operations executive had rallied the troops over the last few hours and shared the long list of crises that were impacting the overall business. It certainly sounded like an organisation that was convulsing from all the challenges. He concluded, "Clearly we have lots of issues, our business disruption plans were non-existent, almost none of our managers had a clear plan of action for the next week, and everyone is scurrying around, blaming others to protect themselves in the event of a mass retrenchment."

Storm held his head, berating himself for not driving his team harder to prepare for an emergency and create clarity when it was called for. They should have anticipated this. After all, that is why he paid them a good salary. When the operations executive was done, "Clearly, you all contributed to this mess. I want a detailed report on the actions you will take to get us back on track and make up for the losses we have just incurred."

As each senior leader walked out, their unspoken words were probably similar: they disliked their boss, hated the working environment, had no clear view of what needed to be done, and wondered who amongst them might not have a job in a week. The overarching feeling was fear, which only added to the chaos. It was clear they would still be firefighting for a while.

Story 2: Resilience and clarity

Terry was reviewing some strategic reports when there was a knock at his door. One of his up-and-coming high performers was standing there. Terry beckoned her in, "Morning. I can see you have something on your mind. What is it?"

She sat down and showed Terry an early hurricane system alert, "Sir, this is the big global weather system we knew would come one day. Based on our analysis, we believe it will arrive within a week. Fortunately, we have planned for such an event in our scenario planning. We need to pull the trigger to activate the emergency response."

Terry studied the information for a few minutes. "Great work. I concur that we need to pull the trigger."

Terry picked up his mobile and called each of his executives, alerting them to the anticipated hurricane system and urging them to activate the crisis response plan immediately. He smiled as he recalled the simulation exercise they had run a few months ago. Initially, it was met with scepticism, but in the end, everyone enjoyed it and appreciated its value. This, however, was the real thing.

He walked across to one of the conference rooms and observed that the head of strategy had already activated the crisis response war room. *Nothing like being prepared*, he thought to himself. He sat at the table watching the strategy executive take the response lead role. He went through numerous key actions, tested understanding, and allocated key activities to selected individuals. After three hours, he nodded to Terry, "I think we are ready." He nodded back in agreement. It was already early evening when Terry drove home for a family dinner.

By mid-morning the following day, it was clear that Impact Inc. was prepared to deal with the ramifications of the hurricane system. Everyone knew the risk of the potential damage and disruption, but there was a definite sense of reality and preparedness. It was also clear that there was nervous anticipation, but nobody was panicking.

Comforted that his team were on top of the crisis response, Terry headed to his office and used some quality thinking time to plan for the key building blocks required to move the business beyond the short-term ramifications of the hurricane that was barrelling towards them. He knew that the team was resilient and would handle the immediate actions, but he focussed his energy on the courageous steps required of him and his leadership team. Once he had a broad sense, he called in a cross-functional group to share his thinking and to challenge the bold actions they may need to take. With some tweaks and an addition that he had missed, they agreed on the key milestones. Roles and responsibilities were assigned, and everyone clarified expectations of each other.

With about one day to go, it became clear that they were ready and able to respond to most of the anticipated challenges. He connected with each of his executives to assess final preparations. A few of them wanted to continue for another shift. Terry made a gutsy decision and sent everyone home to prepare for the hurricane and to safeguard their families. They also ensured that each employee had a buddy system of three colleagues. He was concerned about some steps he was taking, but when he received several texts of appreciation, he realised it was the right call.

Once the hurricane hit, the buddy system kicked in, and Terry followed up to ensure that each employee was contacted daily. Once the storm subsided, various leaders agreed it was safe to return to work. Remarkably, they had nearly full attendance after the disruption. Within two days, Impact Inc.'s business was fully up and running.

Terry also received heart warming feedback from various operations where managers had boldly supported local communities that could not fend for themselves. Given their preparedness, they even acquired new customers, who were speedily supported.

When the Executive Team met a week after the hurricane, Terry began by thanking them and giving recognition to those who had demonstrated resilience during the week. They also reviewed how they had responded, what had worked well and where they could improve. They concluded it was not perfect, but their preparedness had given them an advantage amid the crisis. Terry then reviewed the additional building blocks that would get them back on track and recover lost ground. Everyone agreed wholeheartedly. Terry sat back, proud of the team he had the privilege of leading.

MINDSET SHIFT 11

Disengaged → Engagement and communication

Question: Do you embrace frequent two-way engagement and open communication?

Key mindset transition: Shifting from being disengaged, having a culture of fear and negative energy, to engagement, communication and voluntary, discretionary energy.

👀 Observations

	Disengaged	**Engagement and communication**
Expressions (what we hear)	• Absenteeism and many complaints. • Disparate efforts in silos. • Silent quitting.	• Be the message, not the messenger. • Leaders are transparent in their communications. • Regular updates and feedback.
Behaviours (what we see and feel)	• Employees are disengaged. • Employees feel undervalued. • Employee opinions are disregarded.	• Communicate expectations and test for understanding. • Leaders engage at all levels. • Positive attitude to engagement.
Ways of working (what we experience)	• Critical issues are slow to surface. • Corridor talk is destructive. • Mediocrity and poor performance.	• Listen & solicit input. • Open to challenge/ feedback/engage. • Effective cascading of messages.

🔑 Key message

At the time of writing, global statistics indicate that only one-third of the world's employees are engaged, while approximately two-thirds of the workforce are disengaged or actively disengaged. Within this context, employee engagement is a strategic imperative and requires regular dialogue, interaction, and communication. The significance of that level of disengagement provides a huge opportunity to turn latent effort into value creation. After all, you are paying their salaries, so you should engage them in a meaningful and productive way. Disengaged employees are a drain on profitability, so why keep your employees in the dark? Keep them informed, energised and engaged.

Employee engagement is a critical two-way process that ensures that both parties connect and seek mutually beneficial outcomes. Effective engagement creates an emotional connection, encouraging employees to bring discretionary energy and positivity to the workplace. When people are engaged, they are more willing to go the extra mile, do more, reduce mistakes, focus, and produce their best work. Gone are the days of telling only, as this limits you to what you know. Openness to two-way communication expands opportunities, ideas, inclusivity, and diversity of thought. When people understand the "why" of their jobs and are contextually aware, they can add to the organisation's efforts, rather than detract from it. Importantly, it also drives top-line revenue and bottom-line profitability.

Equally, communication is an important leadership task, as it ensures the dissemination of vital information to employees, so that they are informed appropriately. Whilst simplicity in communication is important, the level of detail depends on circumstances. On the contrary, too much communication can dilute its impact. Again, the bottom-up communication flow is essential, as it keeps leaders informed and ultimately leads to more robust decision-making.

Getting people to share stories is a powerful way to engage and communicate. In Trillion Dollar Coach[11], it is said, "The simple communication practice- getting people to share stories, to be personal with each other – was in fact a tactic to ensure better decision making and camaraderie."

Other practical considerations for improving employee engagement could include, a conducive work environment, work-life balance, learning, growth opportunities, team effectiveness, and recognition.

Key pitfalls for leaders to avoid in employee engagement are not listening, failing to take action and not providing appropriate support. The positives from employee engagement can quickly be negated if employees do not see and experience tangible change.

Key principles for engagement and communication, extracted from *Your Leadership Footprint.*

- Transparency and authenticity from leaders.
- Consistency and frequency of dialogue and engagement.
- Soliciting inputs, concerns, and questions.
- Being open to challenge.
- Sharing relevant information.
- Providing timely feedback on critical matters.
- Delivering on promises and commitments made.

👣 Practical steps

Effective employee engagement can take many forms, including:

- Frequent employee check-ins.
- Stand-up meetings.
- Focus groups or leader-led dialogues.
- Townhalls.
- Employee engagement platforms.

ⓘ Warning signals that a shift is required

- A culture of fear is prevalent throughout the organisation.
- Employees are disconnected, disengaged, and low morale is prevalent.
- You hear about critical issues from third parties, often after it is too late.
- Disengaged employees are leading to significant staff churn.

📖 Anecdotal business examples

Over time, I've done many lessons learned reviews. This type of review seeks to find the root cause of an event and document lessons that can help improve business performance. These are often triggered by significant negative outcomes or failure within organisations. When I am called in to help such organisations, I am also told that they have a middle management or supervisor problem, which was the cause of the failures experienced. Consistently, a culture of fear is a core root cause, and noticeably emanates from the most senior leaders. A culture of fear inadvertently encourages a good news culture, resulting in major issues or losses being covered up. The reality is that they have a leadership issue. The problem almost always starts at the top.

I also often observe organisations where employees are disengaged. When there are high levels of disengagement, you may be paying them a salary, but the likelihood is that you probably receive less than half of the true energy you are paying for. When employees are disengaged, they underperform, become silent quitters, fail to innovate, lack motivation and are probably looking for another job. Employee engagement is often overlooked, but can be a source of tremendous energy and value.

> **Business issue for the two stories: Digital transformation project**
>
> *Reminder: As explained in the introduction, the two stories are told as opposite extremes of the mindset transition. Leaders should understand the tensions between the two extremes and find a balance that best fits their context or situation.*

Story 1: Disengaged

Brash Inc. was about to embark on a significant digital transformation journey, and the CEO, Storm, was preparing the capex request for Board approval. The organisation's track record in capital projects was dismal, often because of poor project leaders. Storm had already decided to appoint Travis, a tough-minded operations leader, who could get the job done. He anticipated resistance from the Board, but was prepared to push back.

The capex request for the digital transformation project was met with scepticism at the Board meeting, especially given past project failures. As usual, Storm was belligerent in demanding the approval of the capex, stressing the criticality of progress on digital transformation. He stated, "Failure to move now on the digital project risks putting us far behind our competitors." The debate about the project leader was rather heated, but Storm was pushy and finally got the capex approval and agreement for Travis to run the project.

As the project progressed, it soon became clear that the team members were not meeting performance hurdles. Storm was becoming increasingly agitated by the slow progress. Much to his annoyance, the Board had demanded an external review, which indicated that the project team were disengaged. In discussions with Travis, he concurred that the external findings were nonsense. They agreed to drive the project and team more ruthlessly.

Storm joined Travis in several project meetings to demonstrate support and to ensure that it was a show of force. Slowly, the reports began reflecting positive trends and encouraging results. Items flagged as risk items were either taken off the register or mitigated. After a few meetings, Storm stopped attending, confident that Travis was enforcing tough project disciplines.

During the six-monthly investment committee meeting, Storm sat back smugly, knowing that his decision on Travis was delivering results and that he could afford to push back at some members who had been quite vocal a few months ago. Most members were subdued in their response to the digital project report and feedback. One member indicated that the report and his observations from other meetings did not align. Storm was dismissive, pointing menacingly at the hefty report in front of the member.

As the months passed, the project reports showed positive news, despite no visible impacts on the business from the digital transformation project. Storm also became aware of several resignations, but decided they clearly could not keep up with the pace of an intense project. He also spoke briefly to a project member who mentioned that the project overruns were limiting his work stream. On enquiring about the overruns, Travis waved it away nonchalantly, stating that the individual was misinformed.

Storm had been advised of a key digital launch event and had diarised it. As the date drew closer, Travis was non-committal and subtly suggested a postponement, citing an enhancement which would make the launch even more impactful. Several weeks passed, and despite the continued positive project reports, no tangible or physical results from the project were visible. Travis remained buoyant and insisted that he was driving the team hard.

Being aware of the upcoming investment committee, Storm went to the dedicated offices where the project team was housed. It was late afternoon, and he expected to see the project office buzzing. Instead, he was met with a rather muted project office, with most desks empty. The few team members in the office avoided eye contact and appeared glued to their computer screens. Storm engaged one junior and asked, "Where is everyone? How is the project going?"

The junior staffer shrank into his chair, "I don't know, sir. I don't think I'm allowed to say anything."

Storm was enraged and demanded, "What time do people leave here daily?" The junior shrugged his shoulders and sank even further into his chair. Storm realised he was not getting answers and returned to his office. He called Travis, but the call went straight to voicemail. He left a message, insisting that Travis come and see him immediately.

Travis called back a while later and apologised, stating he was meeting a service provider to chase up some delivery aspects. Storm asked, "Travis, I need you to tell me that the project is going well, because I don't have a good feel about it."

Travis replied, "Hey Storm, a few minor hiccups, but everything is on track. We lost some time, but I know we will accelerate and make our overall milestones." Storm wanted to accept it, but he could not help but feel something was amiss."

Storm looked up, surprised that the Chair had walked in and dropped a report on his desk. He said, "Storm, this is the independent report on the digital transformation project. There is a complete disconnect between what you are reporting and what the independent review has found. I have called for an in-depth committee meeting with all parties involved."

Storm had gone pale and struggled to reply, "Sure."

Story 2: Engagement and communication

Terry was reviewing the capex request for Impact Inc.'s digital transformation project. He was impressed with the quality of the submission and the proposed team. He was comfortable with Frank, who had been proposed as the project leader, knowing he easily engaged people and got exceptional results from a project team. He also knew that Frank consistently kept his promises and was realistic about setting and meeting expectations. He was a natural project leader.

Terry had invited Frank to the investment committee, wanting members to be comfortable with the project leader. They jointly presented the capex proposal, which was well received. One member raised his hand and asked, "The plan looks great, but can we accelerate it by three months?"

Terry nodded to Frank, trusting him to respond. Frank politely shook his head, "Yes, it is possible, but given the nature of the digital solutions we are putting in place, I would not recommend it. If we miss any key digital coding, we could create unnecessary risk for the entire project. Hence, I would rather temper those expectations now than bring back bad news later." The member nodded and gave a thumbs-up signal. Terry smiled, aware that he had the right project leader in place.

Soon after the project was approved, Storm received a request to allow for a team effectiveness intervention. Frank indicated that the project team needed to be aligned and engaged upfront, as this would help set up the team for success. Terry knew the value of engagement and immediately gave his approval.

During the first few months, reports indicated slow progress, and Terry was surprised by the project team's candour in admitting mistakes and how they learned from those mistakes, which would help them in the future. Although slightly concerned, Terry trusted the process and openness from Frank and the team.

With the upcoming six-monthly investment committee meeting, he headed to the project offices where the digital transformation project team was housed. Even though it was late afternoon, he was pleasantly surprised by the positive energy that filled the room. People looked up, greeted him, and smiled. He stopped at the desk of a junior staffer and asked, "How is the project going?"

The junior smiled and replied, "Well, sir, we had some challenges, but our leader has been actively engaging us, and each day feels like we're making greater strides. I feel that we're now on a positive trajectory. I am also loving the learning that this project is giving me. It makes me want to give more discretionary energy. I don't want to let the team down."

Terry smiled and shook his hand, "Well done, it sounds like success to me." The junior smiled and returned to his computer screen.

Terry looked around for Frank and eventually spotted him actively engaged with a team. Terry ambled over, wanting to remain unobtrusive. Frank saw him and beckoned him over, "Hi Terry. Please come and join us. Some of our team members are engaging with an ecosystem partner. We believe some of our early failures have led to a key breakthrough." Terry nodded and stayed at the back of the small group. The level of engagement and positive communication was clear.

Terry walked in for the second launch demo that had been planned. The previous one had been good, and the team had brought the second date forward by over a month. The reports for today had been conservative, and Terry expected only minor changes from the previous session. Frank's team seemed excited but presented poker faces. He wondered what was going on. Frank asked everyone to be seated and handed it over to his team. They demonstrated many new solutions, tools, and enhancements. Terry was very impressed and stood to provide a round of applause. This got everyone up, cheering loudly.

Terry remained standing and thanked the team for their dedication and hard work. He could sense that the team were fully engaged and had a sense of belonging. Terry felt a hand on his shoulder and was surprised to see the Chair standing behind him, "What is the secret that led to the project's success?"

Terry replied, "We should ask Frank, but from my perspective, it is a few things: appoint the best possible project leader, give them a clear mandate, focus on team effectiveness, create a transparent culture and allow for open communication. The rest of the project should then take care of itself."

The Chair looked Terry in the eye, "I guess our next committee meeting is going to be a breeze."

MINDSET SHIFT 12

Disconnected and misaligned → Shared purpose and aligned

Question: Is everyone aligned to a shared purpose that unlocks discretionary energy?

Key mindset transition: From disconnected and misaligned to unlocking discretionary energy through a shared purpose.

👀 Observations

	Disconnected and misaligned	Shared purpose and aligned
Expressions (what we hear)	• Negative corridor talk. • I'm looking for another job. • I'm the boss, just do it.	• We hear "why" we are doing it. • Clarity of messaging and impact. • Talk of a bigger purpose.
Behaviours (what we see and feel)	• Lack of commitment and disconnected. • Low energy levels. • The tone from the top is poor.	• Positive energy and stories. • Emotional support for "why" • Passion for making a difference.
Ways of working (what we experience)	• Lack of energy. • No clarity on "why" • Efforts are disparate and muted.	• Commit to meaningful work. • Positive towards change. • Seek to unlock discretionary energy.

🔑 Key message

Achieving alignment between a shared leadership purpose and individual purpose encourages individuals to connect emotionally to the organisation and do meaningful and impactful work. When employees' hearts and minds are aligned to a shared purpose, they are more likely to bring discretionary energy to their work, which drives greater outputs and achieves superior results. Great leaders shape a shared purpose that emotionally connects the "why" for the organisation and individuals.

It is important to note that shared purpose is why people want to connect with the team or organisation, whereas a corporate purpose expresses why teams or organisations exist. In my leadership facilitation work, I often introduce team alignment and liken it to winning the World Cup. This encourages them to think big and makes the concept of alignment more impactful. A great example of purpose and shared purpose is the Springbok rugby team, which has won many World Cups. Although their objective, to win the World Cup, was similar to every other competing nation, what ultimately separated them was their shared purpose, to win for the country. Their emotional connection was to something bigger. This unlocked discretionary energy and produced the extra effort, which saw them rise above others and win the World Cup.

Shared purpose creates an emotional connection to something bigger. It also brings role clarity, meaning to work, improves engagement and drives up motivation. This is significant because individuals want to belong to something bigger than themselves, seek meaning in their work and belong to something where they can make a difference. I often extend this concept of a shared purpose to leaders, helping them clarify their leadership "why" and their obligation to show up as leaders. The magic sauce is giving people reasons to go to work and contribute meaningfully.

The biggest challenge leaders grapple with is getting the shared purpose cascaded to all levels of the organisation, especially customer-facing employees. Senior leaders understand it, but it needs to be obvious to everyone if it is to unlock the potential of the whole organisation.

In Simon Sinek's book, Start with Why[12], he says, "People don't buy *what* you do, they buy *why* you do it." The same philosophy applies to unlocking talent energy. It is easier to ignite the fire of passion in people when they know why they are doing something. In the absence of why, when things or circumstances change, individuals will generally struggle to adapt, because while they may understand the what, they might not understand the why.

Practical steps

Selected guidelines for defining a shared purpose (extracted from *Your Leadership Footprint*);

- It must explain the "why" in the context of a team.
- The narrative must be clear.
- It must align with individual beliefs and values that shift the mindset and attitude.
- It must enable individuals to self-direct their actions, efforts, and decisions.
- It must accelerate the execution of mutually agreed-upon outcomes.

Warning signals that a shift is required

- Few people can articulate a shared purpose or why they are in a team.
- Low staff morale.
- Teams are lacklustre and show little energy.
- Staff churn is high, with many people looking for other jobs.
- Discussions in corridors are overly negative.

Anecdotal business examples

Disconnectedness or misalignment is prevalent in many organisations and manifests when individuals or teams follow their own agenda. This can occur because of individuals or through unintended organisational architecture. By unintended, I mean either poor implementation of the operating model or not thinking systemically about how the different parts need to work together. I've observed that poorly established ways of working can be value-destroying. Another widespread observation I have in organisations or teams is the lack of unity around a shared purpose, as defined earlier in this chapter. When people do not connect to the "why", they underperform, fail to execute, and frequently deliver poor results. Teams then start to compete against each other, do their own thing, become messengers, and few can articulate why they exist or how they align teams. This often leads to disengaged people who do the bare minimum. Sadly, this is true for too many teams or organisations.

I once facilitated a leadership intervention for an organisation, which included crafting a shared purpose that loosely spoke about the leaders' role in infusing energy and using it to unlock the potential of people and the organisation. The second day required an activity to be completed. Many of the leaders, quite frankly, did not show up and demonstrated poor leadership behaviours in the moment. At the end of the activity, I reflected on what I had seen and asked, "If your employees had observed what I just witnessed, how would they have experienced your shared leadership purpose?" That powerful learning moment was pivotal to the leadership team and created an enormous shift in how they subsequently showed up.

Business issue for the two stories: Team alignment

Reminder: As explained in the introduction, the two stories are told as opposite extremes of the mindset transition. Leaders should understand the tensions between the two extremes and find a balance that best fits their context or situation.

Story 1: Disconnected and misaligned

Brash Inc. had experienced a rollercoaster ride over recent years, with multiple shareholder changes, a rotation of leaders, and market challenges. The Board believed they had found the perfect leader in Storm. He was highly assertive and demonstrated the toughness needed to stabilise the business.

Storm wasted no time calling his Executive Team in and laying down clear rules of engagement. In his first executive meeting, he conveyed a clear message: "The Board has given me free rein to stabilise Brash

Inc. However, I want to make this clear: we are going to fix and grow this business in record time. To achieve this, I will create stiff competition amongst you as my team. Maybe putting some fire under you is more appropriate. I expect your teams and business units to do whatever it takes and to show double-digit improvement within six months. My intention after six months is to keep only the top performers. The rest will have to find new jobs." Storm glared at shell-shocked faces, "Are there any questions?" He was met with a stony silence.

Storm spent the next few weeks mulling over how to structure an incentive system to create the competitiveness he sought. He believed that if his Executive Team competed more in the market, everyone could win. He knew holding individuals accountable for performance was the quickest way to success.

As the months rapidly ticked by, Storm became increasingly infuriated by the lack of results and, in fact, deteriorating performance. Executive meetings became shorter, increasingly frustrating, and there was mostly a one-directional demand for results.

As despair settled in for Storm, he became aware of a significant contract, where Brash Inc. was included as a potential vendor. He called for an urgent sales meeting with the executives of his two largest business units. Storm started the meeting by making it clear that Brash Inc. had to win the contract at all costs. He asked for the views of his executives. Nobody was forthcoming with any concrete steps, but they agreed that due to their products and available production capacity, Brash Inc. was best placed to win. One of the executives also suggested that if the two business units competed in the market, it would increase the likelihood of winning the contract. Storm hastily agreed and asked to be kept abreast of progress.

Pondering over another poor set of results, Storm was startled when his phone rang. One of his executives excitedly announced, "Great news, boss. I have won the contract."

Storm was over the moon. "Great news indeed. Just make sure we get started immediately; we need our production to ramp up." Storm sat back, gloating, *about time*, he thought to himself. Still smiling from the news, he texted his golf buddies to organise a game for the following afternoon.

Storm was looking forward to the monthly executive meeting and anxiously awaited the detailed reports, which he demanded be sent out at least three days before the meeting. This would then give him ample time to consider tough questions that support his driving style of accountability. He shouted to his assistant outside his office, "Where are the reports for the Thursday meeting?"

She skulked into the office, "I've been chasing them since yesterday. There was a server issue. We will get the reports a day late." Storm scowled and waved her out. He made a mental note to grill his team for this unacceptable delay.

When he finally received the reports, he went straight to sales volumes and was pleased to see a jump in the top line. *This is more like it*, he mused. His eye immediately went to the bottom line, and the smile rapidly escaped from his face. It reflected a substantial loss. Just below the bottom line was a note in bold that indicated this was due to start-up costs, and results should be substantially up in the coming months. Despite the loss, he felt encouraged that they had turned the corner.

At the meeting, Bob, the executive whose business unit had won the contract, was brimming with confidence, whilst the rest of the team appeared rather dour. Storm used the meeting to heap praise on Bob, reflecting that he was indeed on his way to success. Thabo, the financial executive, cleared his throat to talk, but Storm silenced him, "Let's enjoy our success." He turned to the rest of the team, "I hope this serves as a good reminder of what is possible, so best you get on and deliver the results we agreed to."

By the financial half-year, the results showed a dogged determination to maintain the loss despite improved volumes. Storm had started to realise that the sales price in their contract may not be the best. He had asked an external consultant to do comparative market pricing on their contract. When he opened the report, the harsh reality of his supposed crown jewel contract was laid out quite clearly. The winning contract price was probably twenty per cent below market rates. Storm dropped into his chair, a feeling of despair gripping his body. The internal competition he had driven so fiercely had destroyed Brash Inc. financially. Increasing prices now would require a monumental effort.

Story 2: Shared purpose and aligned

Impact Inc. had experienced a challenging period, with multiple shareholder changes, a rotation of leaders and market challenges. The Board had deliberated hard and believed they had found the perfect leader in Terry. He was assertive but demonstrated the emotional intelligence needed to engage people and drive a sustainable business.

Terry took time to understand the business and wrap his head around the complexity of the cultural nuances that had been part of Impact Inc.'s legacy. He quickly realised that his senior Executive Team was disconnected, misaligned, and lacked energy. As he reflected on this, he realised that the root cause of the issue was not external, but internal.

Terry understood that he needed to tackle the misalignment differently, and that he had to start a journey with the team, and not impose himself with a demanding leadership style. He engaged an external facilitator and created an approach that he believed would shift the dial for his leadership team.

He arranged for his Executive Team to spend a couple of days off-site, to align on what they needed to do to improve results. The team unpacked the context and quickly realised that they were fundamentally misaligned, and this cascaded into their teams, resulting in substantial under performance. The facilitator guided them in establishing a shared purpose. He explained that a shared purpose would create meaning for individuals and teams and drive discretionary energy. As the executives grappled with the concept, they started to internalise what it meant, and as the first day ended, they realised that it could be a game-changer for them collectively.

Terry supported the team as they aligned behaviours and ways of working to collaborate more effectively as an organisation. The shared purpose was the glue that held them together, but also encouraged accountability. One of the executives used the analogy of winning the World Cup. They could win together if each took individual accountability and supported collective ownership.

Executive meetings were strained at first, but as time elapsed, it was evident that there was elevated alignment and more open support for the shared purpose. As a team, they started seeing green shoots of positive results and success stories. Terry increased his visibility across the business and both advocated and showed support for broader alignment.

A few months into his tenure, he was informed of a substantial contract, which had the potential for a step change at Impact Inc. Terry assembled his leadership team to discuss a strategy for winning the contract. Whilst it was obvious that Impact Inc had a competitive advantage, it was by no means a guarantee. Bob, who ran their biggest business unit, stated that it was past practice for Impact Inc. business units to compete for such contracts. There was immediate tension in the room, and a few leaders shifted uncomfortably. One of the executives asked, "Does that not conflict with our shared purpose?"

Terry immediately acknowledged this, "Great challenge. I agree we need to be aligned and work towards our shared purpose. How are we going to do this differently?"

Even though he wanted to go it alone, Bob realised this was a pivotal moment for the organisation and his team. "I agree. If we are going to win our own World Cup, we need to respond to this contract opportunity differently." After a few hours of deliberation, they agreed to work together and deploy people from across the business units to a collective contract bid team.

Aware that the contract winner was to be announced, the Executive Team gathered in the corporate office coffee shop. Although there was apprehension, there was also excitement. Bob's phone rang, and he slowly picked it up. He listened intently for a minute or two, keeping a poker face. He ended the call and looked at his colleagues, "Great news, we have won the contract. The client will award us the contract, but would like to see some concessions for community projects. Well done, team." Everyone cheered and dished out handshakes and fist pumps.

Terry was preparing for his monthly executive meeting and reviewed the short but focussed monthly report. All the indicators were going in the right direction, and bottom-line results were glowing. Terry opened the meeting, "Firstly, I want to applaud a team effort. Our shared purpose and alignment resulted in winning as a team and organisation. Secondly, if our results continue trending this way, we can all look forward to handsome rewards." The team all looked at Bob and gave a brief round of applause.

Bob nodded and replied, "This was a team effort. I will invite the bid and production teams to a celebratory lunch. After all. It takes a complete system to win a World Cup."

PART C

TEAM

Mindset shift 13: Stifling talent and limiting people ➜ Nurturing talent and unlocking potential

Mindset shift 14: Lack of clarity and disarray ➜ Framing and context

Mindset shift 15: Stagnation and missing opportunities ➜ Open-minded, curious, and innovative

Mindset shift 16: Favouritism and exclusion ➜ Embracing diversity and inclusion

Mindset shift 17: Conflict and defensiveness ➜ Constructive challenge

Mindset shift 18: Silos and wasted duplication ➜ Collaboration and seeking synergy

MINDSET SHIFT 13

Stifling talent and limiting people → Nurturing talent and unlocking potential

Question: Is your team actively growing and nurturing talent?

Key mindset transition: From suppressing people to finding the gold in people and unlocking their full potential.

👀 Observations

	Stifling talent and limiting people	Nurturing talent and unlocking potential
Expressions (what we hear)	• There's no time for training. • It's not my idea, so I won't do it. • People should develop themselves.	• Encouraged to grow & learn. • "How can I help you grow?" • Let's leverage our strengths.
Behaviours (what we see and feel)	• Paying lip service to the development of others. • Not listening to understand. • Telling others what to do.	• Proactive learning culture. • Open to innovation/ new ideas. • Encourage curiosity from others.
Ways of working (what we experience)	• No time & budget for training. • Failure is seen as weakness. • People are denied opportunities. • Perfection and fault intolerant.	• Growing future-fit capabilities. • Support the growth, exposure, and development of others. • Seek to find the potential of each person.

🔑 Key message

People are the only real asset of any organisation; they make everything happen. Importantly, people or human capital can appreciate in value over time. A key leadership role is to find the gold in each person, nurture them, grow them and unlock their full potential. As a leader, you can create an environment where every human being can flourish, bring their best efforts, dedicate their energy, shine, and be given opportunities, which unlocks their latent human potential. I assure you that nothing is more fulfilling than watching someone rise and fulfil their potential, because you did something to make it happen. You would have delivered on the privilege of being a leader.

Below, I reflect on two aspects of nurturing, namely: finding the gold and seeking passion, and two of unlocking potential, namely: a learning culture and future-focussed capabilities

From a nurturing point of view, I want to emphasise the notion of finding the gold in each person. On our leadership journeys, we often meet individuals who have never stepped up or been given opportunities. This means nobody has taken the time to dig deeper and mine for the gold. Each of us has gold – talent, strengths, ideas or capabilities – but all it takes is for someone else to be intentional in seeking the gold in them.

Secondly, nurturing entails seeking what people are passionate about and playing to their strengths. As a leader, if you can align an individual's passion with work that needs to be done, you are more likely to get exponential results. Being deliberate about understanding strengths means you can match capability with work to be done, leading to increased engagement, motivation and outputs. It also helps them set higher expectations for themselves, which becomes a self-fulfilling prophecy. In psychology, there is a concept termed the Pygmalion effect, when higher expectations lead to improved performance. The more you give someone the belief of greater expectations, the more likely they will deliver.

From an unlocking potential point of view, leaders need to create an environment that supports a learning culture, curiosity, innovation and learning from mistakes. A learning culture requires leaders to go first and

109

set the tone from the top. A learning culture also focuses on asking open-ended questions.

Secondly, unlocking potential entails developing your talent for future-focussed capabilities. With the pace of change in the world today, skills rapidly become outdated. Therefore, focussing on building future-ready capabilities is fundamental and requires leaders to think about and sense what those future skills will be. Finally, I believe talent development should emphasise building innate human abilities such as curiosity, innovation, imagination, intuition and creativity.

The concept of unlocking potential is expounded in The Extraordinary Leader[13], where they quote Martin Seligman, "I do not believe that you should devote overly much effort to correcting your weaknesses. Rather, I believe that the highest success in living and the deepest emotional satisfaction comes from building and using your signature strengths."

Practical steps

Selected considerations for nurturing talent.

- Using empathy to put people first.
- Engagements with people are focussed on how you can unlock their full potential.
- Creating a conducive environment for success.
- Understanding your employees' strengths and passions, and seeking to enhance those.
- Encourage learning and self-development.
- Find opportunities to provide recognition and feedback that builds up.
- Seek opportunities to mentor and coach.

Warning signals that a shift is required

- Performance management focuses on negatives.
- Employees have limited growth opportunities.
- Talented individuals do not stay long.
- There is no support for learning and development.
- Individuals are boxed into roles, without engaging them.

📖 Anecdotal business examples

When I conduct leadership interventions, I always get a leader to do a team analysis based on diverse criteria. There is often an individual who comes out unfavourably, showing up as "red". The natural disposition is to want to move or get rid of the person. I then give them a thirty-day challenge to change the person to a "green". I encourage them that this is the real work of a leader, unlocking energy or potential, even if they hold a strong view of the person. I encourage them to start with a one-on-one conversation and be intentional about seeking to turn the person "green". I have been pleasantly surprised that most people who use the challenge have successfully turned the person around, and more interestingly, the average turnaround time is twenty-one days.

Benjamin Zander in the book *Art of Possibility*[14] talks about giving someone an A. I have taken the concept slightly further in the leadership development work by encouraging leaders to start with A+ and then being deliberate about finding the gold in the individual to support the A+. A university tutor attended one of my workshops, applied this philosophy and achieved a fifteen per cent improvement in results for his entire student group in less than twelve weeks. I encourage you not to miss the next opportunity to try this. I also have numerous similar anecdotal examples.

> **Business issue for the two stories: Talent management**
>
> *Reminder: As explained in the introduction, the two stories are told as opposite extremes of the mindset transition. Leaders should understand the tensions between the two extremes and find a balance that best fits their context or situation.*

Story 1: Stifling talent and limiting people

It was a blustery Monday morning, and Storm groaned as he checked his diary. He loathed the talent workshops, which Brash Inc. ran twice per annum, led by the human resources executive. He sensed that his Executive Team shared his dislike of the topic. Therefore, only a handful of senior leaders were invited. He did not want to waste people's time, and frankly, he would rather be elsewhere.

Priya, the human resources executive, started the talent workshop by sharing the latest feedback from the employee engagement survey. The results were rather dismal, particularly the data related to career growth and the lack of opportunities. Storm was quite vocal, "Why can't they just be grateful that they have jobs?" A few of the team nodded in unison.

Priya bit her tongue and was about to retort, but knowing the audience, she chose to ignore it. She then outlined details related to staff churn and resignations in senior and middle management ranks. One of the executives jumped onto this, "Clearly, we have a flight risk across our management levels. We should increase salaries and tighten our performance management discipline."

Another executive added, "I also think some of these networked teams we started are creating unnecessary tension. I strongly feel that we should push people back into their boxes, so they can focus on doing actual work." The workshop deteriorated rapidly from there, and many executives fuelled the debate with negativity about how useless some employees or functions were.

Storm ended the meeting early, "I think we've heard enough. I need HR to step up and stop the flight risk. Send out an email about it." Priya nodded softly, but inside she was fuming and frustrated. She realised again that the CEOs EQ limited the business. She was clear about what Brash Inc could do to change the flight risk narrative, but she felt powerless because Storm had limited her influence and ability to take corrective action.

Sitting at his desk, Storm formulated a stern email to all the management layers. Why bother waiting for HR, he thought to himself. He kept the email short but emphasised that the management layers were well paid, and it would be senseless to change jobs because of money. He also stressed that the business must stamp out this flight risk dialogue that was circulating. Satisfied that the message would send a strong signal, he pushed send on the email. He also looked at the pile of training requests, which had been on his desk for weeks. In frustration, he pushed them to the bottom of the pile.

As Priya returned to her office, her staff looked up in hope, knowing nothing would change. The look on her face conveyed the same sad message as before. The little remaining energy in the team slipped from the room. She avoided eye contact and quietly closed her office door.

She sat down, head in her hands, wondering whether the fight was worth it, or whether she should embrace the flight risk narrative and look for another job. She picked up the employee engagement report and read the comments supporting the poor scores. She felt nausea crawl up her throat, realising that she could not stand up to Storm and challenge how they were stifling their talent and limiting their growth opportunities. She felt guilty, praying that somehow, she could gather the strength to tackle the CEO and some of her executive colleagues.

Over lunch, some of the HR team huddled together, whispering discontent as they prepared the annual performance management process, which was to be circulated the next day. What should have been a positive human resources activity was feared because of the culture of using the performance management process to punish employees for purported poor performance. The feeling of remorse about their involvement impacted each of them. The mood was dampened even further when one of them announced their resignation. "You're lucky", said one of them. A sentiment many shared, but few voiced.

Driving home the next day, Storm noted that he had received no responses to his email of the day before. It niggled him somewhat, but by the time he got home, he had convinced himself that the message had landed, and the silence implied that everyone was in agreement and would take appropriate action.

Sleep evaded Storm for a few nights, increasing his frustration levels. His wife confronted him over dinner, "I sense your anxiety. I would guess it probably relates to people. If you want to perform as a CEO, you must take a softer approach towards people." Storm grunted. She replied, "You know I am right."

His wife's message gnawed at him for several days. Unable to shake it, he called Priya, hoping they could find a new way forward.

Story 2: Nurturing talent and unlocking potential

As CEO of Impact Inc., Terry made human potential a strategic priority. Early in his career, he had limited exposure to true mentors, and only later appreciated the value of mentoring and having someone look out for you. Once he had grasped the concept and witnessed the profound impact you could make on others, he made unlocking the potential of others a personal mantra. It was core to everything he did as a leader. He understood that a critical leadership role was intentionally seeing each employee for who they are, what they are good at and how they could outperform. All it needs is someone to believe in them and encourage them to fulfil their potential.

It was a blustery Monday morning, but Terry was energised as he eagerly anticipated the quarterly talent day, run by Priya, the human resources executive. It was a key strategic event fully supported by the leadership team. Terry firmly believed that the right leadership would nurture talent and unlock the potential of people. This would positively impact customers, and business results would follow.

Priya welcomed everyone and became aware of the positive energy bouncing around the room. The well-attended talent day represented people from across Impact Inc. As had become tradition, the first two hours focussed on giving recognition to people and sharing success stories. The agenda item for this read, "Gold." This referred to how each leader sought to find the gold in people. This idea of finding gold was now ingrained in Impact Inc.'s cultural DNA. It was no surprise that the career growth and opportunity scores from the recent employee engagement survey were so positive, she mused to herself. This agenda item also asked each leader to name the top three strengths of each direct subordinate. This encouraged leaders to look deeper and consider leveraging their capabilities more effectively. Priya appreciated that her human resources role contributed to developing human potential, the organisation's most valuable asset.

The second item was reserved for the CEO. Terry held a deep belief that leaders need to nurture talent. He tangibly demonstrated this by asking for feedback and enquiring how Impact Inc. could unlock more of the potential of each individual. Terry quipped, "If we unlock human potential, then we can have greater societal impact." This part of the talent day always surfaced robust debate and meaningful feedback. Terry was consistent in his approach; he would listen carefully and commit to action based on the best ideas tabled. Terry was a powerful ambassador for leader-led human capital development.

The remainder of the day would focus on aligning and executing the prioritised ideas. Given the clear mandate of nurturing talent, the topic easily captured the hearts and minds of participants. Terry would always leave these sessions energised and ready to face any challenges the organisation or outsiders would throw at them. He knew that their A+ talent gave them a distinctive competitive advantage.

Following the completion of the talent day, the human resources executive and her team would prepare for the quarterly development discussions. These focussed on integrating some of the talent day actions with meaningful mentoring conversations focussed on the development of individuals. These discussions were always a deliberate two-way conversation focussed on leveraging strengths and unlocking their employees' passion. Adopting a development approach translates into improved business results and ultimately performance deliberations. This differed from most organisations, which would focus on deficiencies and gaps. Priya believed these discussions should focus on the ninety-five per cent that was going well, rather than the five per cent that may not be perfect.

Terry had a standard question on the Executive Committee (EXCO) agenda following the talent day. He would ask his Exco whether they fostered a conducive environment for people to succeed. The intent was to ensure that his Executive Team were always aware that they were the custodians of the environment, which led to organisational success. It was a deeply reflective, honest and fruitful conversation. It also highlighted their visible role in attracting and retaining talented people.

Over the following weeks, Terry and Priya took pleasure in reviewing and approving learning and development opportunities for their people, knowing that any investment in people would build their human capital and ultimately yield rich dividends. It was even more satisfying when they saw individuals seize the opportunity, shine and grow.

MINDSET SHIFT 14

Lack of clarity and disarray ➜ Framing and context

Question: Do your leaders spend time on framing and creating context?

Key mindset transition: Shifting from biassed assumptions to framing the narrative that unlocks business value.

👀 Observations

	Lack of clarity and disarray	Framing and context
Expressions (what we hear)	• I don't know what they want. • We were caught by surprise. • Stop questions, just get it done.	• Narrative that provides clarity. • Leaders asking powerful questions. • Leaders providing clear context.
Behaviours (what we see and feel)	• Clarifying questions are not allowed. • No clarity on next steps. • Hidden agendas and game playing.	• Leaders listen to understand. • They tell stories to clarify. • They encourage ideas from others.
Ways of working (what we experience)	• Context of key actions unclear. • Questions are vague. • Assumptions become fact.	• Leaders tell the story. • Questions are encouraged. • Everyone is clear on context.

🔑 Key message

Leaders play a critical role in framing the strategic objective and creating an appropriate context for others. This is important as leaders have a holistic view of what action is required in a particular situation. I often observe that leaders have thought about an idea or concept for a while, and they therefore believe that others intuitively get what they have been thinking about. Do not assume that everyone knows what is in your head. It may be obvious to you, but it may not be obvious to others.

Hence, framing is important. You need to connect the dots for your teams so that execution can be optimal. In the absence of this, people may interpret an expectation in their own way and make assumptions which may not necessarily be correct. Without strategic thinking, framing and leading change, execution is hampered and unlikely to deliver effective results. Framing also reduces cognitive biases in thinking and decision making. It guides thinking to the real strategic objective or problem being solved, reducing wasted time and effort for individuals to unravel the requirements.

In my previous book, *Your Leadership Footprint* (question 10.1), I refer to framing powerful questions. As a leader, framing a powerful question can change perspectives, spark creativity, ignite passion, kindle innovation and create a paradigm shift in mindsets.

Framing and context require a few essential steps:

- Framing the problem statement as a powerful question.
- Applying quality thinking time to the framing question.
- Defining what we are solving for and what great would look like if we are successful.
- Being aware of the context and adopting an outside-in view.
- Articulating the narrative of what we seek to achieve, articulating the value, impact, the why and the desired outcomes.
- Engaging others, seeking inputs and ideas, socialising and getting support.
- Challenging each other about how it can be done differently.
- Encourage action and provide support.
- Give recognition and celebrate success.

Framing and context highlight important leadership behaviours and expected ways of working to drive success. These could include active listening, asking open-ended questions, expecting questions in return, clarifying expectations, testing understanding, providing support, learning from mistakes and being open-minded. Importantly, don't forget to give recognition when due.

Closely linked to this is owning the strategic narrative. This allows leaders to shape and own the narrative that drives an organisation. The key is to convey a high-impact story that explains the "why", clearly articulates the ask of everyone, and provides momentum for action.

Practical steps

- Be clear in framing the objective.
- Provide adequate context and clarify expectations.
- Allow clarifying questions and test for understanding.
- Articulate the story or narrative which guides thinking.
- Provide support for action and execution.

Warning signals that a shift is required

- Actions and responses to issues are unexplainable.
- Biassed assumptions hold sway in conversations.
- Questions to leaders are frowned upon.
- In moments of crisis, responses are slow and uncertain.
- People are unclear on what is expected of them, and they don't clarify.
- The story being told differs from what leaders intended.

Anecdotal business examples

The absence of framing and context was once demonstrated in a client in a most unproductive way. A Board member asked a particular question, and as questions were frowned upon, the executive responded that he would revert with a prompt response. He then mobilised a team, who worked through a weekend to produce a 100-page slide deck. When presenting the report, the Board member was surprised. He said, "That is not what I was asking". Then, with a simple clarification question or two, the executive provided a twenty-word response. Wow, what a waste. All because the executive did not ask a clarifying question.

Many years ago, I was involved in a small manufacturing business for the mining industry. Production was sub-optimal to say the least. One of the challenges for the general manager was the emergency requests for specific products, many of which were bespoke. These emergency requests were passed to the production floor, disrupting the factory and increasing worker frustration. When someone eventually intervened, framed the situation and created a context for the supervisors, a solution was quickly found. This is a simple example, but it resulted in a tripling of production units within two weeks.

Business issue for the two stories: Organisational effectiveness

Reminder: As explained in the introduction, the two stories are told as opposite extremes of the mindset transition. Leaders should understand the tensions between the two extremes and find a balance that best fits their context or situation.

Story 1: Lack of clarity and disarray

Storm pondered what one of his golfing partners had mentioned over the weekend. They had undergone an organisational effectiveness programme which embedded their new operating model. He did not listen to the specifics, but it sounded like a great idea. Brash Inc. struggled after making a few selected changes to its operating model. His perspective was that they were great ideas, but his team had just executed them badly. Maybe some organisational effectiveness would be the solution to the challenges they faced.

He got his assistant to set up a Teams call with a friend who was a freelance management consultant and Thabo, his finance executive. After some idle chatter, he said to the consultant, "I've heard great things about organisation effectiveness, and I think we need some real effectiveness at Brash Inc. Our business units are struggling with the operating model changes I made, and quite frankly, they need some provocation to get things going. You're a management consultant, can you help us with this? Of course, you know I don't want to overpay for this work."

The consultant replied, "Yes, of course I can help. When do you want me to start?"

Storm replied, "The sooner the better. I'll give my team a heads-up, and you can start next week." Thabo was about to interject when Storm cut him off, "Let's chat offline. You can come to my office after the call."

Storm had a broad grin on his face when Thabo walked in. He chirped, "I think a bit of a shake-up and a few actions on organisational effectiveness will be good for us, don't you agree?"

The finance executive paused, immediately realising that he could not speak his mind, so he opted for a few questions: "Storm, don't you think we should have prepared a clear scope, followed our procurement guidelines, and obtained formal responses to a request for proposal. I'm concerned about the approach we took in appointing the consultant."

Storm laughed, "Don't stress, I've known this consultant for a long time, he knows his stuff and won't charge us a lot. Let us not waste time when the solution is obvious. Please email the Exco team and advise them that the consultant will spend a few weeks with us. I would appreciate their full cooperation." Thabo's shoulders dropped as he walked out.

A few days later, the finance executive was cornered by some of the Exco team, "What is this organisation review all about? We need to get better clarity. We assume from the email you sent that we're in for a further round of cost-cutting." All they got was a shrug of the shoulders.

When the consultant arrived at their offices the following week, each Exco team member had made their own assumptions on interpreting the organisational effectiveness review. Within days, the review was labelled as a significant cost reduction. Naturally, the barriers went up, and the consultant was unable to engage effectively or have meaningful discussions with anyone. It also didn't help that the consultant was unclear about his mandate.

Late on Friday, Storm passed the consultant, "How are things going? I would imagine that by now you have quite a few improvement actions."

The consultant nervously nodded, "Yes, there's a lot of complexity here, so I don't want to jump to premature conclusions. By next week, we should have some firm ideas." Satisfied, Storm turned, looking forward to a Friday night dinner with friends.

A similar pattern played out over the next two weeks, with limited progress from the consultant. Each Exco team member was preparing for cost cuts and juggling thoughts about whom they might let go. By now, Storm was anxious and annoyed at the lack of progress and clear results.

After five weeks, Storm called for an urgent Exco meeting to discuss the organisational effectiveness review. After receiving feedback from the consultant and each of the Exco team, Storm slammed his fist into the desk, "This is ridiculous. I wanted to review our effectiveness, and now each of you is making dramatic cost cuts in your business units. How did this go wrong?"

Silence entered the room, and nobody was prepared to go first. Eventually, Thabo plucked up the courage to respond, "I guess we were not aligned with the intent of the organisation effectiveness review. I certainly wasn't clear."

Priya, the human resources executive, added, "In hindsight, this is a classic example of a failure in clarity, which led to disarray. As you implied, Thabo, we need to frame the organisational review better and provide greater context. Sadly, we have drained energy from the organisation. We have work to do to regain our credibility."

Storm stared in disbelief, even more frustrated than before, "OK, maybe we need to stop whatever we have done and start again." Without realising it, many of the Exco team let out a deep sigh of relief. Storm knew he was to blame for the lack of clarity. He had a hollow feeling, recalling a similar situation from his early career. He should have known better.

Story 2: Framing and context

Terry was engaging with fellow CEOs at an industry breakfast, sharing ideas for value creation. One of his peers mentioned running a highly effective organisational effectiveness review, which had helped them cut out excess waste in their business. Terry was curious, and by the end of breakfast, knew that this would be valuable for Impact Inc., as they were always looking at how to become more effective.

Terry caught up with Thabo, his finance executive, and they researched what was achievable. After further input from the Exco team, they issued a request for proposal to three management consultants. The request was clear: help Impact Inc. find opportunities for effectiveness by eliminating waste. The request also made it clear that it was not a cost-reduction exercise. Numerous other criteria and design principles were identified and included in the scope.

While Terry waited for the proposals to be returned, he engaged broadly with the Exco and the business units on the objective of the organisation effectiveness review and his expectations to unlock more value and drive meaningful work. As he shared his thoughts, he clarified expectations and tested for understanding. He also confirmed what resources the business needed and what time was freed up to make the review impactful, but not frustrating. He sensed clear support across the leadership teams. Importantly, everyone had clarity about why the review was being conducted. This ensured that participation would be focussed, biases would be managed, and nobody needed to waste time thinking about unsubstantiated rumours.

Once appointed, the consultants had a clear mandate and knew exactly where to prioritise their efforts. They shared simple frameworks that quickly pointed conversations to the unseen waste in the business. Various focus groups were conducted using an agile methodology, and within the first week, there was a strong sense of where opportunities lay for driving simplicity and effectiveness. All the leaders had a clear view of what needed to be done and were equipped with a summary of frequently asked questions, which allowed them to respond to questions and concerns in the moment.

By Friday, the end of the first week, the consultant walked over to Terry's office and said, "I believe that we've had a productive week, and it is clear that your leaders and the business are aligned and willing to work collaboratively. I think we will get to tangible actions quickly. Have a great weekend."

Terry smiled and nodded, "You too." He was grateful that their commercial process ensured they found a consultant with fit-for-purpose experience.

The following week, Terry joined one of the focus groups to see firsthand what was happening in the project. As he sat, he noticed discomfort on the faces of some of those in the room. He responded quickly, "I want to clarify that I'm merely observing. You must share whatever is on your mind, as you are closer to the business than I am." The consultant picked up on the cue and asked a few thought-provoking questions. As the ideas started flowing, the team quickly became oblivious to the CEO in the room. Terry observed with interest how the consultant stood back and assessed the entire business system, identifying patterns and connecting the dots. Terry was sitting quietly, taking notes as ideas came to mind, pleased that the organisation effectiveness review was showing tangible progress.

By the end of the second week, progress was confirmed with tangible actions which, when executed effectively, would free up executive time and unlock value for Impact Inc.

Terry called his Exco together in the third week and allowed the consultant and their internal team to share their initial findings. By thinking systemically and reviewing the not-so-obvious, several review processes involving executives and senior management had been identified as wasteful and not value-adding. The Executive Team analysed the feedback and decided collectively to eliminate the identified waste immediately. The finance executive smiled, "Wow, our collective decision has probably saved ten per cent of the time for our top fifty leaders."

Terry applauded, "Well done, everyone. Even if we only implemented this one recommendation to eliminate waste, it would be worthwhile. The freed-up leadership time can be refocussed to value-adding solutions"

Without being prompted, the consultant and an executive presented more feedback. Terry was surprised; there were other tangible opportunities to eliminate waste across the management layers, their meeting effectiveness and selected ways of working. He smiled, satisfied that the framing and context setting had been critical in setting up the review for success. He would sleep well tonight.

MINDSET SHIFT 15

Stagnation and missing opportunities → Open-minded, curious and innovative

Question: Do you encourage questions, open-mindedness and curiosity?

Key mindset transition: Shifting from being closed-minded to taking people on a journey of discovery.

👀 Observations

	Stagnation and missing opportunities	Open-minded, curious and innovative
Expressions (what we hear)	• Why change what is working. • No involvement and participation. • I'm too busy firefighting to fix this.	• There must be a smarter way. • Let's apply system or design thinking. • Fail fast, fail forward.
Behaviours (what we see and feel)	• One-directional communication. • No tolerance for mistakes. • Reactive and slow.	• Encourage innovation and new ideas. • Allow crucial conversations. • Use mistakes as learning opportunities or teachable moments.
Ways of working (what we experience)	• Questions are viewed as opposition and resistance. • Challenge is not permitted. • Little urgency for making things happen.	• Challenge assumptions and think constructively. • Invest time to take people along and explain objectives. • Recognise the value of external inputs and questions.

🔑 Key message

As you have gathered from some of the earlier mindset shifts, leaders play a critical role. In being open-minded, curious and innovative, they need to lead from the front. Being curious is an enduring leadership quality, which implies lifelong learning, an imperative in a rapidly evolving world. When you are open-minded and curious, you accept that there is always a better way of doing things. The tone starts at the top. If leaders do it, then others will follow, and vice versa. Leaders must be intentional about asking open-ended questions and actively listening. This paves the way for a learning culture and an innovative organisation.

Building on the idea of a learning culture is an extract from The Extraordinary Leader[15], "Innovative leaders were also good at learning from both their successes and failures", and "A key to being innovative is increasing one's ability to learn." This echoes the earlier point that the tone starts at the top.

Organisations should also be intentional about thinking through their business and understanding what is holding back learning, curiosity and innovation. Common areas of disconnect in organisations include the operating model, self-imposed business silos, poor cross-functional or business collaboration, counter-intuitive processes, complex systems or burdensome governance mechanisms. Leaders should consider these to understand how they limit opportunities and value creation. I sense that in organisations, a significant amount of value is trapped because of this leadership mindset.

Making space for quality thinking time (QTT) is critical for curiosity and innovation. QTT is a value-enhancing function and requires action. You need to be deliberate about making time to think. Sadly, in my engagements with leaders, very few have the time to think. If you are not thinking about what might be different in your organisation, then who is?

Psychological safety is important for a curious and innovative organisation to thrive. Leaders must create an environment where courageous conversations, constructive challenge and robust debate are strongly encouraged. No single person has all the answers, and the safer it is to challenge, the more resilient your organisation will become. It is also important to note that often the most innovative ideas come from outside your organisation, and sometimes even from another industry.

Practical steps

- Allow time for innovation in the normal working day.
- Hire curious people and inspire curiosity within your workforce.
- Allow for creative thinking time where people can create solutions.
- Encourage learning on the job.
- Identify and support individuals for growth opportunities.
- Remove business processes that block experimentation.
- Lead from the front on curiosity.

Warning signals that a shift is required

- Open-ended questions are not allowed or heard.
- Nobody listens to ideas or suggestions.
- Mistakes have punitive consequences.
- Your business bemoans a lack of innovation.
- Leaders with egos are never challenged.

Anecdotal business examples

The resources sector is a classic example of boom-and-bust cycles. In a declining cycle, they often go through two classic stages, a downward cycle and a restructuring cycle. In the downward cycle, they limit initiatives, cut investment and introduce austerity measures. This is followed by a restructuring cycle with huge changes, retrenchments, and driving organisational paralysis. It is intriguing how organisations do not learn from previous cycles, repeating the same common mistakes, with the same negative unintended consequences. The focus becomes extremely narrow, and my experience is that management is so busy with firefighting that they are closed to new thinking, which could reduce the impact of the current crisis and prevent this from happening again.

I recently worked with a large multi-national organisation who were very open-minded, allowed questions, wanted feedback, encouraged challenges and explored new ideas. This combination of behaviours and ways of working proved to be a catalyst for new thinking, new ways of doing things and trying new things. Within a year, they fundamentally changed the business, resulting in record business results. The critical success factor was the CEO and the Executive Team who led the strategic change required. They appreciated how their open-mindedness was pivotal in unlocking value.

Business issue for the two stories: Innovation

Reminder: As explained in the introduction, the two stories are told as opposite extremes of the mindset transition. Leaders should understand the tensions between the two extremes and find a balance that best fits their context or situation.

Story 1: Stagnation and missing opportunities

Storm was stewing as he read the analyst report sent to him by the Chair. The headline shouted, *Brash Inc. has stagnated and missed crucial market pivots*. Naturally, he was defensive about Brash Inc's achievements and closed the report. Storm felt they had reasonable results in a tough market and scoffed at the idea that the young analyst understood their business. As far as he was concerned, analysts were a drain on good business practises and always had a pessimistic short-term view of the world. After all, he had been at the helm as CEO for many years and knew the business inside out.

The Chair also requested them to discuss why Brash Inc. had missed a key market pivot at the next Board session. This irked Storm as he liked to be in control and did not enjoy being dictated to, whether by an analyst or the Board. Pushing back his frustration, he spent some time preparing his defensive reasoning on why they had avoided and missed a key market shift. He was confident they had made the right decision and believed it was merely a temporary market trend. He felt they needed to consider the long-term, and missing one pivot was not stagnation.

During the next Board session, the Chair outlined some thoughts about the market pivot and wanted to understand the rationale for a cumbersome response and, quite frankly, a missed opportunity. He concluded his opening commentary, "It would seem that consumer trends have shifted, and that they are not only buying more products online, but they are also far more aware of the environmental impacts of packaging. Please explain to the Board why we missed the key shift and believe this is not a permanent market shift."

Storm confidently waved a thick report at the Board members seated around the table. "This research from a few years ago indicates that consumers will still buy in-store. I have studied this, and I firmly believe that the hype caused by online shopping will die down and people will revert to physical shopping in the next few months. I predict that the online stores will disappear before the end of the year. I had a small team look at the online option, and frankly, their views were not credible. We must stick with an approach that has served us well for decades."

Many Board members were aware of how Storm would challenge them if they raised too many questions, so they often left with questions that were not asked. One of the new members quietly asked, "What about the packaging issue?"

Storm jumped in quickly, "Just some environmentalists shouting the odds, with no real understanding of what happens in the real business world. Of course, we can simplify the packaging, but let's be honest, consumers love buying the big box and showing it off in their trolleys. I don't think they worry or care about how many goes into the packaging. Besides, we get lucrative volume discounts from our packaging supplier." Storm felt pleased that he had held firm and quietened the dissenting voices.

The Board member was not backing off, "I sit on another Board, where they have innovated the packaging. Their market share is up. I think Brash Inc. may have missed an opportunity."

Storm was about to respond when the Chair intervened, "Storm, I would encourage you and the team to do some market research with your current consumers and see what they want. I have a similar gut feeling that we're missing an opportunity." Storm nodded but offered no reply.

A few weeks passed before the Chair's final comment surfaced in Storm's thoughts. He walked over to his marketing executive and stated, "Maybe we should check in with a few consumers and see if they're really into this whole online shopping thing."

The marketing executive looked down and softly replied, "No need to check in, our sales are down twenty per cent, and most of that has gone to online competitors. We've stagnated, and someone else is enjoying our lunch."

Annoyed, Storm stated, "And the packaging issue?"

Feeling intimidated, the marketing executive opened a drawer and held out a funky box, "This is what our long-term rivals have done. Consumers are loving it."

Storm held the box, surprised and unable to say a word. As he turned to leave, he muttered under his breath, "I suppose we had better call an urgent meeting; we may have to make some tweaks to how we do business."

The marketing executive rolled his eyes at the disappearing CEO. *If only he had listened two years ago.*

Story 2: Open-minded, curious and innovative

Terry looked up as one of his colleagues entered, "Hey Terry, it seems like the analysts are happy with how we have responded to key market shifts over the last while. It was reported on one of the online business websites this morning. Well done!"

Terry replied, "Thanks for sharing. Remember, it was a team effort. However, what's far more important to me is what we do as a business and how responsive we are to customer demands. I'm glad the analysts are finally seeing what we have seen for a while." His colleague nodded and left his office. Terry returned to his preparation for the Board meeting.

The Chair had requested an open debate on market shifts and how Impact Inc. might respond in the future. Terry had briefed his team, who caucused customers, tested with marketing insight thought leaders and analysed the data against their sales. Terry always appreciated how his team stepped up and focussed on the business, rather than just working in the business.

During the next Board session, the agenda item on market pivots came up. The Chair congratulated Terry and a few additional executives who had been asked to join the Board meeting for this agenda item: "Well done on how the team and organisation have responded to the online market opportunities." He generously gave them a round of applause. Looking at Terry, he asked, "What market shifts or opportunities are you seeing that we can take advantage of?"

Terry pointed to his team, "Let them respond, as they are closer to the customers than I am." The team duly responded with thoughts on new opportunities and happily answered clarifying questions from the Board members. It was apparent that they had a solid understanding of customer needs and expectations.

As the Chair was about to close the agenda item, a new member asked, "How are you responding to the shifts in packaging which have been driven by environmental awareness?" One of the Impact Inc. team replied with a clarifying question. The member elaborated on what he had seen in engaging with another unrelated organisation regarding changing trends in packaging.

Terry realised they had not fully explored the packaging issue and jumped in, "To be honest, we had not considered it from that perspective. We will have a small team investigate it immediately and explore how we can innovate, address the environmental challenge, and collaborate with our customers to create an opportunity for value add. This should also reduce wasteful packaging. Thanks for that contribution." With everyone in agreement, the agenda item was closed.

The following day, Terry walked over to the marketing executive, who smiled, "Don't worry, I already have a team working on it. I'm sure we'll make a few mistakes, but with our ability to innovate, we will make improvements and realise opportunities soon."

Terry smiled, "Great, exactly what I would have expected. Shout if you need me to free up resources, budget or capacity. In addition, maybe the two of us should visit a few key customers and get their views." The marketing executive nodded in agreement.

Within two weeks, the team had made great strides, but not before making a few mistakes and "failing fast" as they called it. They had a prototype ready for Terry and the marketing executive to take to customers. They had pre-arranged several customer visits, and the overall response was positive. One of the last scheduled visits did provide a surprise. One of their largest retail customers, who was sarcastic, provided a profound insight and suggested a change in the packaging, which he felt would be more useful and value-adding. Terry replied, "Thank you, we appreciate the feedback and will certainly consider your suggestions. They make sense to me."

Driving back to the office, the marketing executive could not hide his excitement, "Do you realise that the suggestion we just received is both genius and will save us a few per cent in costs. These visits and being open-minded have given us yet another opportunity to retain our market-leading position." Terry held up his hand and gave his colleague a fist pump.

Within days, new product offerings and packaging were rolling off the production lines. Terry smiled, realising that their curiosity and agile approach were paying dividends and allowing them to keep pace with the rapidly changing consumer environment. He looked forward to the weekend away in the bush with his family.

MINDSET SHIFT 16

Favouritism and exclusion ➜ Embracing diversity and inclusion

Question: Does your team embrace diversity and inclusion?

Key mindset transition: Shifting from favouritism and exclusion to creating a sense of belonging where everyone is included and valued for their diversity.

👀 Observations

	Favouritism and exclusion	Embracing diversity and inclusion
Expressions (what we hear)	• Discrimination and shutting people out. • Frustration. • Nepotism.	• We're interested and value diverse views and thinking. • Let's hear all the voices. • Diversity is seen as a competitive advantage.
Behaviours (what we see and feel)	• Discourage points of view. • Preferential treatment for some. • Absence of trust.	• Listening to all perspectives. • Including everyone in discussions to get input. • Positive morale and work climate.
Ways of working (what we experience)	• Window dressing. • Sink or swim approach. • Inconsistent application of performance management.	• An environment where people from diverse groups can succeed. • Free knowledge sharing by all. • Intentional support and accelerated learning opportunities.

🔑 Key message

Diversity and inclusion can be an emotive issue in any workplace and cause conflict because of personal beliefs. When you simplify the intent behind diversity and inclusion, it becomes apparent that it fosters a more conducive environment for sustainable success. Diversity means being open to everyone and their thoughts and perspectives, regardless of age, experience, race, gender or ethnicity. Inclusion means everyone is respected, welcomed, supported and involved. Both are essential to driving a human-centred organisation where we put people and humanity first.

From an organisational point of view, unlocking the business's full potential means tapping into the talent of every human being. There is no logic in only tapping into the energy, ideas, thinking and capabilities of a handful of people. On the contrary, by leveraging everyone, you open up a complete perspective of the world, customers and employees. If you exclude some people, you may miss significant opportunities.

While much is made of diversity based on individuals and personal traits, I believe the opportunities can be unlocked through diversity of perspective and thought. We tend to see the world through a very narrow view based on our lived experience. The picture only becomes clear when we bring all the different views together, and we can see the full potential of context, challenges and opportunities. By not considering the diversity of perspective, you may venture into a project, product or service with blind spots, which could derail you.

From my perspective, inclusion ensures that everyone is valued, feels included and delivers their best efforts. Elsewhere in this book, I refer to global levels of disengagement. This often emanates because people feel excluded. Quite frankly, there is no point in employing and paying employees, only for them to be excluded, disengaged and give you the bare minimum effort in return. It is value-accretive to engage and tap into the potential and discretionary energy of everyone who works for us.

Leveraging a pragmatic approach to diversity and inclusion will create an environment for perspectives, ideas, innovation, creativity, growth and development. It is also important to realise that if you do not create such an environment, your best people may leave to find an organisation where they might have a sense of belonging.

In Trillion Dollar Coach[16], this is well summarised: "Great people flourish in an environment that liberates and amplifies that energy. Managers create this environment through support, respect and trust."

👣 Practical steps

Selected practical steps to drive diversity and inclusion

- Uphold core values regardless of context or person.
- Ensure that teams have diverse representation to ensure the leveraging of perspectives.
- Encourage diversity of thought.
- Review workplace practices for the inclusion of all employees.
- Unlocking the potential (finding the gold) of each person creates a competitive advantage.

⚠ Warning signals that a shift is required

- Favouritism towards selected groups.
- Different perspectives are not accepted.
- Certain individuals or groups are marginalised.
- Groups or teams are biassed towards certain people.

📖 Anecdotal business examples

Given my work in leadership and culture, the stark contrast between organisations that leverage diversity and inclusion, versus those that do not, is glaringly different. I have observed that leaders who are more attuned to diversity of perspective and are inclusive are more responsive and generally more profitable. Conversely, organisations that do not promote diversity and inclusion are often stuck, mostly in crisis, losing talent and are on a downward profit trajectory. What fascinates me is how organisations can be inward-focussed and not see the obvious thing that holds them back. This includes openness to external views. As a management consultant, I may often hear, "You don't understand our industry." While this may be true, a different perspective could shine a light on opportunities or defects.

One of the unintended consequences of management or organisational structures is that people who are similar rise to the top, are often older and therefore become relatively biassed in their perspective of the market, people and the organisation. Sadly, this can lead to value leakage. I have observed that organisations that are intentional in designing to counter this weakness will often reap significant rewards for doing it differently. Examples could include collaborative cross-functional teams, employee councils representing a cross-section of employees, and ensuring diversity of thought by introducing opposites into dialogue or debates. This intentionality often brings innovation, new opportunities and enhanced value creation.

Business issue for the two stories: Diversity and inclusion

Reminder: As explained in the introduction, the two stories are told as opposite extremes of the mindset transition. Leaders should understand the tensions between the two extremes and find a balance that best fits their context or situation.

Story 1: Favouritism and exclusion

Storm was looking forward to the annual strategy breakaway, which was traditionally held in a big five game reserve. Previously, it had been a boys' club for the Executive Team. This year was different, as Priya had joined the team as a human resources executive. Despite subtle hints that she would not enjoy the weekend in the bush with the boys, she was unflinching and set on joining them.

Thabo, the finance executive, was responsible for preparing the strategy and budgets for the strategy weekend, which, in Storm's view, was more of a rubber-stamping exercise, with the real focus being time with the guys. Thabo had set up a series of pre-strategy sessions to get input. Storm saw this as a waste of his time, as he had a clear view of the strategy, who would help them get there and what the numbers should be. Storm always gave Thabo a clear view of what he expected to read in the strategy report.

During the first pre-strategy session, Thabo would share the draft strategy and thinking and invite comments. It was also clear that Storm only really allowed comment or input from his three operational executives, who were also amongst his best friends. Storm did not attempt to disguise the favouritism he showed the operational directors. From the inputs raised, it was evident that group think was at play. Whilst some executives had made subtle comments on this, in Storm's view, it was confirmation that they were strategically aligned. After their inputs, he even chirped, "See, great minds think alike."

During the second session, Priya challenged the Executive Team, "Given how important people are to our business and the execution of our strategy, why do we not include more on leadership, people and culture in our strategy?"

Storm felt the frustration levels rise in his body, more because of the thought of having a woman at the strategy weekend than the actual question raised. Without thinking through his response, he quipped, "Seriously, HR should happen automatically. We shouldn't have to call it out in our strategy." Then, in a slightly raised voice, he looked at the rest of the team, "Right, guys?". With the glaring stare, nobody was going to challenge him.

Priya sat back deflated, contemplating how to elevate the 'People' agenda. It was clear that the cultural awareness of Storm, the Executive Team and the business left a lot to be desired. Another topic she was eager to raise was the demographics of the management team. Many of them were over fifty-five, male and white. One unspoken but widely held view was that only relevant experience in this industry counted. Any suggestions from younger generations were frowned upon and summarily dismissed.

Storm arrived at the bush camp before the others and ensured the beers were on ice. "Priorities", he laughed to himself. As his Executive Team arrived, he welcomed everyone with a high-five and a cold beer. He watched Priya arrive and felt awkward at her being here and ruining the boys' weekend. He offered her a beer, which she declined. "This is going to be interesting", he muttered quietly.

The first afternoon was traditionally spent on a game drive, followed by a boma *braai*, with the strategy workshop the following day. Some executives held back their normal banter because Priya was in the game vehicle. Storm was trying to show off his birding knowledge, only to be corrected by Priya. Storm was irritated, but it quickly became apparent that Priya was a highly accomplished birder. When she showed him a new birding lifer, he was delighted, but not happy that it came from her.

Storm kicked off the strategy session the following morning, looking overly tired after a late night. It was clear that this session was merely a formality. Priya tried raising the 'People' agenda again, only to be stalled by Storm. "Let's not ruin the weekend, Priya. We can pick it up next year." She fumed and realised again that, notwithstanding her executive role, she was not part of the team.

One of his executives, and closest friend, interrupted. "I would like to hear more from Priya on the 'People' agenda." Storm was exhausted from the night before and did not have the wherewithal to argue.

Priya did not need another invitation. She had done her homework and spoke to issues close to each executive's heart. A robust dialogue on people, leadership and culture ensued. Perhaps, she mused, diversity and inclusion may just stand a chance. With the Executive Team agreeing openly with Priya's strategy suggestions, Storm had to acknowledge her determination. He made a mental note to be more inclusive in the future.

Story 2: Embracing diversity and inclusion

Terry looked at the recommendation from his Executive Team for the annual strategy conference. He had a tradition of getting them to nominate where they should go. This year, they had selected a small bush lodge not too far from the city. He approved and gave his assistant the go-ahead to make the reservations. He had also suggested they include two people who were not from the Executive Team, as he wanted some differing voices in the room. One was a highly talented female manager, and the other was from their youth council.

Thabo, his finance executive, agreed to coordinate the pre-work that went into the strategy workshop. Terry felt that if they were to spend two days away, it should be well spent, which meant comprehensive preparation. Although Terry had applied quality thinking time to the strategy and shared his strategic thinking with the team, he felt it was important to be inclusive in obtaining input, and he strongly encouraged diversity of thought. Although only two extra people were invited to the weekend away, he ensured broad representation in the strategy pre-work sessions. One of his favourite questions was, "What are we not seeing or considering in our strategy?"

Terry strongly advocated for creating psychological safety, allowing everyone to speak freely, ask questions and contribute ideas. He firmly believed that this had helped them build a more robust strategy and ultimately given them a competitive advantage in the market. He enjoyed watching people contribute and how experienced members of his team encouraged and coached at the same time. Terry had fostered a very open environment, which allowed ideas to flow freely.

During one of the pre-work sessions, Priya raised key questions about whether they were doing enough on the 'People' agenda, and she also challenged the Executive Team on greater gender representation across the leadership levels. The team agreed, and Priya undertook to share recommendations at the strategy session. Terry looked at the youth council member who would join them at the strategy conference, "I would like you to present at the conference and give us a perspective on how our strategy works for the youth internally and whether we are doing enough for our younger customers." The young man smiled broadly, agreeing to engage the youth council and formulate a presentation.

Terry always liked to get to the venue ahead of the team to ensure everything was in order and everyone was welcomed. His assistant had also prepared a small personalised welcome pack for everyone. Once everyone had checked in, they got straight to business and used the first afternoon to set the context in preparation for the key strategic decisions that needed to be firmed up the following day. Terry tested whether everyone was comfortable with the agenda and that no critical issues had been left off. Everyone was aligned.

Once the work was done, they set off for an afternoon game drive and enjoyed a relaxing evening around the boma fire. Terry leveraged the relaxed mood around the boma fire, asking everyone to share something of their life story. This exercise contributed to effective diversity and inclusion, which was critical to the team effectiveness of Impact Inc. Priya smiled at the end of the evening. Even though she was pushing for more on the 'People' agenda, it was clear that Impact Inc. was already well on track.

Everyone was up early for a short bush walk, followed by a hearty breakfast, under a huge acacia tree. Terry welcomed them to the second day, encouraging each to be present and contribute fully to the team effort in finalising their strategy. The session flowed well, and several key decisions were agreed upon. It struck Priya that when the diversity of thought from vastly different experiences was harnessed, the richness of thinking, ideas, solutions, and decisions was enhanced. This was amplified when it came to people matters, and again she was awestruck at the passion for people and diversity.

After lunch, the youth council member presented, leaving everyone gobsmacked. He was eloquent and offered a perspective on the business that no one had considered. Terry congratulated him and approved additional funds to explore some of the concepts suggested. Terry added, "I am glad you could join us. Your inclusion was invaluable. Our future will be in good hands." The young man beamed as he took his seat.

Driving home the following morning, Terry reflected on a successful strategy conference and was pleased with how the team engaged and were inclusive. The business was in good hands.

MINDSET SHIFT 17

Conflict and defensiveness ➜ Constructive challenge

Question: Does your organisation allow courageous conversations that challenge the status quo?

Key mindset transition: Shifting from conflict and defensiveness to constructive challenge.

👀 Observations

	Conflict and defensiveness	Constructive challenge
Expressions (what we hear)	• The loudest voice gets its way. • Defensive and excuses. • That will never work.	• Diverse input from everyone. • There are no bad questions. • "How can we build on that?"
Behaviours (what we see and feel)	• Go into detail to prove them wrong. • Culture of fear. • Hockey stick responses.	• Create a safe space for constructive dialogue. • Encourages, inspires, and infuses energy. • Accept discomfort if questioned or challenged.
Ways of working (what we experience)	• Defensiveness and working in silos. • Lack of information sharing. • Poor decisions are executed.	• Constructive and robust debate. • Tough questions accepted. • Create psychological safety where dissenting voices are heard.

🔑 Key message

Leaders play a critical role in fostering an environment for constructive challenge rather than perpetuating defensiveness and working in silos. The more leaders encourage constructive challenge, courageous conversations, and robust debate, the more resilient and healthier your organisation will be. A quote from Steve Maraboli, "Challenges in life can either enrich you or poison you. You are the one who decides," can help us consider how we approach constructive challenge. It is a choice.

Allowing constructive challenge is often achieved by encouraging open-ended or clarifying questions. One of the most fundamental benefits of allowing constructive challenge is to prevent costly mistakes, poor judgement or poorly considered decisions. We have all seen examples of a headstrong leader who has a strong view and then makes a bad decision. In hindsight, many could see the flaws in the decision, but were too scared to raise concerns or ask questions. Allowing constructive challenge is vital because nobody has all the answers, and being open to challenge ensures the robustness of thinking, objectives, and executable action plans.

The benefits of constructive challenge are improved solutions, quality of thinking, better decisions, more effective execution, enhanced customer experience and a better employee experience.

Open-ended or clarifying questions can be profound in terms of their value-adding potential. A few such questions could include:

- Help me understand your thinking on this topic?
- Help me understand how you got to or tested your assumptions?
- Help me understand what I may have missed?
- How will we know the idea worked?
- How will we measure success?
- How will it be valuable?
- What are the unintended consequences of such a decision?
- What should we stop doing?
- What must prove to be correct for those assumptions to be valid?
- What obstacle do we need to remove to achieve success?
- Have we tested this with customers or considered an external view?
- Is the decision logical and intuitive to explain?

Closely linked to constructive challenge is robust debate. When organisations have a culture that encourages challenge and there is psychological safety, it paves the way for strong deliberation or dialogue. This is important because it is better to have an early, robust debate than to have to fix the mess afterwards. Hence, do not avoid robust and healthy debate, but embrace it with integrity and respect. It is also important to note that there should be no consequences for asking questions; otherwise, the best ideas may never surface.

Whilst constructive challenge is two-way, and mostly encourages bottom-up engagement, it is also important for courageous conversations, which are downward. Many leaders prefer to avoid these conversations or conflicts with colleagues or subordinates. These discussions take courage but are likely to make the biggest impact. Suggestions for courageous conversations are reflected in the practical steps below. It is important to note that courageous conversations drive greater commitment, performance and outcomes.

👣 Practical steps

Following a five-step process encourages courageous conversations

- Intent – be clear on intent by sharing the "why"
- Listen – listen actively and invite different perspectives.
- Understand – seek to understand through open-ended questions.
- Feedback – provide open, honest and constructive feedback.
- Action – agree on corrective actions and accountability.

ⓘ Warning signals that a shift is required

- The loudest voice wins.
- The challenge is not culturally accepted.
- The most senior person decides everything.
- Culture of fear is pervasive.
- Overall dissatisfaction is evident in corridor talk.

📖 Anecdotal business examples

I have experienced and observed many examples where a culture of fear is pervasive. Often, a single leader with a large ego is at the centre of the culture. One particular lesson learned review I completed involved a complex project with an ego-led leader amid the challenge. This particular leader's ego was such that he would shut down conflict, drove defensiveness with outlandish statements and micro-managed individuals into tightly controlled silos. This leader honestly believed he was doing the right thing, despite evidence suggesting the opposite. His inability to allow clarifying questions or accept constructive challenge resulted in a significant financial, brand and reputational loss for the organisation.

I have also been privileged to engage leaders and organisations where constructive challenge is accepted and deliberately encouraged. I recently participated in an executive strategy session where we intentionally asked clarifying questions to seek innovation and drive enterprise value. During one of these sessions, an idea surfaced, which initially was shut down, but when the CEO redirected the conversation with clarifying questions, a healthy and robust debate ensued. With everyone being open-minded and allowing challenging questions, an opportunity surfaced that had been hidden from them. The result was several million in bottom-line profit every month. Had it not been for constructive challenge, the value opportunity would have been missed, possibly forever.

Business issue for the two stories: Innovation

Reminder: As explained in the introduction, the two stories are told as opposite extremes of the mindset transition. Leaders should understand the tensions between the two extremes and find a balance that best fits their context or situation.

Story 1: Conflict and defensiveness

Storm reflected on a recent conversation with a shareholder representative, who said that Brash Inc. was losing its innovative edge, as reflected in the downward trend in results. He felt the shareholders were removed from the day-to-day reality he faced, and that they did not appreciate the daily complexities he had to navigate. It irked him that they now wanted a strategy workshop to address the issue and identify opportunities for greater unlocking of value. He was naturally defensive because it felt like the shareholders were sending him signals that they no longer trusted him. He realised he would need to be far more assertive and push back against any interference.

On the day of the strategy workshop, the shareholder representative indicated that it was to be an open dialogue to explore how they could innovate and drive greater enterprise value. The workshop started well with an open-ended question about how to unlock greater value. Storm responded that Brash Inc. was already successful, and that they had tried everything. He added, "I don't think we should change much. Things are going well." He noticed some of his team nodding in agreement.

The shareholder representative was immediately on the back foot and responded, "Yes, but surely we have not thought of everything"

Storm was instantly defensive, "Like what? What do you think we have missed?"

The shareholder representative felt angered by this defensiveness and verbal attack and referred Storm to the detailed analysis the shareholder team had put together. "Let's have a look at the analysis. It indicates margin improvement potential across products and business units. We should focus this conversation on how we unlock the additional margin."

Storm and his team were often frustrated and annoyed by this type of scrutiny, and their natural response was to review the analysis in detail, find errors or challenge assumptions. Today proved to be the same, as they systematically analysed and criticised the data, concluding that it carried many flaws. Storm added, "Given the major inaccuracies, your conclusion of margin improvement is wrong. Honestly, it will never work."

145

The shareholder representative could feel his blood pressure rising, annoyed at the combative mindset that Storm was adopting, and asked, "Surely, there must be a way to unlock value? Have you guys collaborated and worked across the business units to seek new ideas or innovation?"

One of the Brash Inc executives jumped at this invitation to respond, "Listen, we work hard and do our best in each business. Each of us is responsible for growth in our portfolios. If we get distracted by collaborating internally, we will waste our time when we should focus on selling." This was met with stony nodding of heads.

Another executive added, "We are very different, so collaborating for enterprise value will never work." The strategy workshop ended without a single idea or action to take forward. The shareholder representative left bruised and disappointed, whilst Storm and his team felt vindicated and believed they were doing the right thing.

As the months passed, Storm felt some anxiety as the results kept declining, despite pushing hard for performance. With continued pressure from shareholders, he was forced to take action, eventually dismissing one executive whose performance was most dismal. When the new incumbent took up the role, Storm was clear: "Don't rock the boat, just get things fixed and turn this business around."

Within a week, the newcomer to the role came to see Storm. He stated, "We need to make a critical decision immediately. My predecessor was never open to ideas, but they held some flawed views. We have identified a big issue on one of our contracts, where we have been selling at a loss. I am going to terminate the contract and renegotiate."

Storm was about to interrupt when he restrained himself with some difficulty. When he gathered himself, the newcomer continued, "I will allow constructive challenge in my team. This example is enough to make up half the budget shortfall." Given the quantum involved, Storm had no choice but to agree. He realised that the time for defensiveness was gone.

Storm was silent, realising how he had limited the organisation. Change was going to be hard, but it could not be avoided. He began to appreciate why the shareholders showed the animosity they did.

Story 2: Constructive challenge

Terry reflected on a recent conversation with a shareholder representative, indicating that Impact Inc. was losing its innovative edge, as reflected in the downward trend in results. The conversation hit home for Terry, as he realised how complacent his team had become. When he reflected on it, he realised that because the shareholders were removed from the day-to-day reality, they had a different perspective and could see past the daily complexities he had to navigate. This awareness eased his natural defensiveness, and he agreed to run a strategy workshop to address the decline and explore new ideas and innovation.

Terry appreciated how he and his team may have limited value creation because of defensiveness and operating in silos. He also reflected on how the lack of constructive challenge amongst the senior leadership team had become a silent reality. They avoided conflict and had lost the confidence to ask tough questions. He approached the shareholder representative and asked him to chair and facilitate the session.

The shareholder representative welcomed everyone and articulated the intent and expectations for the workshop, which was to identify opportunities and value-unlocking opportunities. He shared a detailed analysis that his team had prepared and invited open dialogue, encouraged constructive challenge and requested open-ended questions. Whilst the dialogue was slow, it quickly gathered pace and a healthy debate ensued. By lunchtime, several opportunities had been tabled. It struck Terry that changing the lens and constructive challenge opened up new possibilities.

In the afternoon session, they narrowed it down and formed two teams, one to argue for and one to argue against. This process ensured robustness and soon flagged additional opportunities, risks and unintended consequences. It was mid-afternoon when someone jumped up, "Listen, everyone. I have an idea that could be a game-changer," He shared the concept and outlined how the solution could drive new revenue. His excitement rubbed off, as it was innovative and unique. When he was done, he encouraged the team to challenge the idea, improve it, and point out errors in his assumptions and thinking. A healthy but robust discussion ensued, peppered with constructive and challenging questions. Terry reflected on the positive energy bouncing around the room, energy that had been missing from Impact Inc. for some time.

By the end of the day, a clear and tangible value unlock opportunity had been formulated, and a strategy activation plan prepared. The opportunity represented a five per cent improvement in margin, which was substantial. The decision to take action was made before everyone left to catch flights.

Terry had been relatively quiet during the strategic workshop, and he realised that by allowing constructive challenge and getting out of the way, people could innovate and create opportunities. He also realised how important it was for a leader not to feel pressured into having all the answers. He reflected on the many positives of the day and realised that the real value was created by asking the right questions. He made notes on the questions that evoked the best responses and prepared an email to share them with the team. Terry also observed that constructive challenge was essential for value to be unlocked. He also noted that robust dialogue was worth its weight in gold.

A few weeks after the strategic workshop, one of his executives entered his office. "Great news, Terry. Our idea, which we shared at the strategic workshop, has been fully implemented. We have resolved all the technical issues, engaged our customers, and sales are increasing. Importantly, our margins will improve by six per cent, which is more than planned."

Terry smiled and shook his hand, "Well done to you and the team." Terry also called the shareholder representative to give him feedback. He added, "Feel free to challenge us anytime."

As the months flew by, constructive challenge and clarifying questions became entrenched as a leadership behaviour and way of working. At first, results trickled in, but soon the sheer quantum of some of the value unlocked surprised Terry and his colleagues. Terry also became aware that defensiveness and siloed behaviour had been quietly dismantled and replaced by collaboration.

Constructive challenge was becoming a mantra and a rallying call to find new ideas, better ways of doing things and innovation. Impact Inc. had recaptured its innovative edge, and for the moment, there was no looking back.

MINDSET SHIFT 18

Silos and wasted duplication ➜ Collaboration and seeking synergy

Question: Does your organisation create an environment where collaboration and synergy can thrive?

Key mindset transition: Shifting from wasted energy to collaboration that unlocks synergy and value.

👀 Observations

	Silos and wasted duplication	Collaboration and seeking synergy
Expressions (what we hear)	• We'll do it our way. • We don't trust them. • It's not my idea, therefore it won't work.	• What is the best collective outcome? • Lots of open questions. • Clarifying questions are encouraged.
Behaviours (what we see and feel)	• Strong us & them mentality. • Pushing personal agenda. • Solutions and effort are duplicated.	• Engage to get broad input. • Finding win-win solutions. • Engage team energy & synergy.
Ways of working (what we experience)	• Key performance indicators that drive silo mentality. • Governance that limits teamwork. • Rigid operating model and artificial silos.	• Structure for well networked teams is in place. • Seamless rules of engagement for collaboration. • Lend a hand to support others to succeed.

🔑 Key message

Leaders play a key role in defining why collaboration is important to organisational success. When collaboration is embedded and seeking synergy is a common goal, results and outcomes can be significantly enhanced. Whilst the environment is important, establishing appropriate teams and ways of working is fundamental.

One of the most common business issues I come across is that of organisational silos. Whilst some are for good reason, by far the most common are silos, which destroy value, drain energy, cultivate complexity and severely limit value creation. Unless there is a solid commercial reason, internal silos should be demolished.

From a leadership perspective, it is also vital to remove obstacles and barriers that stifle collaboration. In a world of increasing complexity and disruption, no silo can be effective in solving complex problems or coming up with integrated solutions. Today, in a VUCA world, collaboration, cross-functional teams and a networked organisation are a business necessity.

Leaders play a critical role in defining the why, the purpose of any team, the problem being solved, the goal, or the solution required for their collaborative effort. In the absence of a shared understanding of why they are working together, it is challenging to expect collaboration.

Cross-functional collaboration does not just happen, as organisations are not normally geared to work together. Leaders must intentionally adjust structures, work routines, processes, decision-making, and communication to build the capability and skills for collaboration to succeed. This concept is supported in Trillion Dollar Coach[17] where they say, "Work the team, then the problem. When faced with a problem or opportunity, the first step is to ensure the right team is in place and working on it." This reiterates that leaders must create collaboration by design.

It is also important to consider how organisations are structured today, focussed on cost reduction and survival. In addition, many business processes are designed to focus on efficiency within the process, rather than the impact on the end-to-end value chain. This inherently makes it internally focussed and narrows the ability for teams to seek synergy and opportunity. In complex environments, it requires different thinking to step back and consider radical simplicity in end-to-end processes.

One exercise I run in workshops is seeking synergy, simplicity, and myth-busting. I deliberately mix leaders to make it cross-functional and cross-business. We agree and select various difficult business issues. I then give them 60 minutes to identify obstacles, agree on actions to improve the business issue, and finally, consider radical simplicity. The results are often impressive, and the myths surrounding collaboration are quickly shattered.

👣 Practical steps

Key considerations in creating a collaborative environment

- Shared understanding of purpose or "why"
- Conducive environment.
- Clear ways of working.
- Appropriate team selection.
- Structural aspects are effective.

❗ Warning signals that a shift is required

- Silos are pervasive across the organisation.
- Collaboration across teams is poor.
- Effort and energy are wastefully duplicated.
- Parts of the business compete against each other.
- Complexity is cultivated throughout the business.

📖 Anecdotal business examples

A frequently observed example in multiple contexts and industries is where, for historical reasons, silos were created and then started competing.

One example of a heavy manufacturing business stands out. Each executive had different performance metrics, their own office blocks, and was deliberate in limiting information sharing, despite being in an integrated manufacturing facility. In conducting a value-based management assessment, I challenged leaders to think differently. After much protest, we eventually took a holistic view of the business. With minimal structural changes, we unlocked a five per cent margin improvement in twelve weeks. The wasted value over the previous decade was eye-watering.

In another example, a large organisation sold commodities through various channels but was encouraged to compete to make the business more resilient. It was believed that this competition was good for the organisation. Through challenging some of the silos, it became evident that the silos were value-destructive because of differing metrics and not considering the value from an organisational point of view. By adopting an enterprise lens, several value-unlocking opportunities were identified and implemented.

Business issue for the two stories: Unlocking value

Reminder: As explained in the introduction, the two stories are told as opposite extremes of the mindset transition. Leaders should understand the tensions between the two extremes and find a balance that best fits their context or situation.

Story 1: Silos and wasted duplication

Storm had just returned from a year-end break and had reflected on how he could unlock greater value from Brash Inc's business. Market forces had placed increased pressure on all their manufacturing and trading operations. His key reflection was that creating healthy competition amongst the business units would spark rivalry, leading to increased sales, margins and overall profitability. He was well pleased with his new strategy and was looking forward to the first executive meeting of the new year.

Once the formalities of the executive meeting had been completed, Storm shared his thinking on the new business model and how the organisational boundaries would create advantageous competition. He made eye contact with each executive from operations and trading to ensure his message had been received. Storm could sense some resistance from his team, but kept on with his narrative of how this would unlock value and make all of them rich.

Storm was utterly convinced and defensive of his thinking, but some executives showed discomfort. Finally, Thabo, the financial executive, spoke up, "I think I understand your strategy, Storm, but I am concerned with how our current key performance indicators and incentives are structured. They don't lend themselves to your thinking."

Without blinking, Storm quipped, "So let's change them to reflect greater weightings for each business unit and individual executives. I think that if everyone does well using this new business approach, we will all benefit." He paused for effect and continued, "Thabo, I'll work with you to fix our metrics."

Over the next quarter, all indications showed that the internal competition and business silos were producing excellent results, at least from the verbal feedback. Feedback to Storm provided positive stories about revenue growth, optimistic customer feedback, and energy across the business. When Storm questioned selected results, Thabo replied that the new approach was still kicking in. "Don't worry, Storm, the results will show a positive jump by half-year."

It was also noticeable how the Executive Team were less aligned and prone to heated debates on actions and decisions that needed to be made. The executives were also significantly more defensive of their business units and teams than before. It was also clear that there was a strong bias in decisions that suited operations or trading functions. The executives assured Storm that it was part of the *healthy competition*, which was now ingrained into the business culture. "Just watch our future results" was a common retort in verbal interactions.

Storm and Thabo had set up a half-year review session for the Executive Team to provide feedback on business performance. Storm had seen the formal results, which reflected some areas of concern. He started the session, "I've looked at our business results, and sadly, they remain disappointing. We've seen a small jump in revenue, but most of the other financial indicators have declined compared to the six months prior. I need each of you to tell me what is going on."

Each of the executives explained the benefits being realised through the new internal business model. Each elaborated on market successes, increased revenue, positive energy, and the improved ability to control their overheads. One executive stated, "Now that we have control of our destiny, we are in a far better position to shoot the lights out." Each one was defensive and had numerous reasons for the negative numbers. This contradicted the narrative. Another said, "Look on the positive side, we won a major new client. Sure, we have lost some margin, but the long-term upside is huge."

When Thabo presented the consolidated results, he was equally defensive about the increased working capital and overheads. In response to Storm's queries, he quickly replied, "I am not concerned, these are merely short-term adjustments. It will all turn positive before year-end." In response to another query, Thabo said the time executives spent on internal issues and cost allocations was normal. It showed their competitive spirit, and that they cared. Storm frowned. One concerning fact surfaced. Two executives had cut their margins to win work from the same client. Thabo was measured in his response, "Well, at least we got the revenue."

Storm reflected on where the business was going and was concerned, but realised it was his idea. He understood he just had to push harder. Once they had all presented, he made a few suggestions for potential synergies. The suggestions were met with muted interest and vague promises to collaborate in the coming months to test whether the ideas could work. When pushed for firm commitments, he was quickly reminded of the impact on the individuals' new incentives.

Storm reluctantly accepted the responses and closed the session, "OK, let's see how this plays out over the next six months. Each of you will have to push harder, especially in your sales."

Over the following months, nothing changed, and results stagnated. Driving home one day, Storm felt enormous chest pains. He pulled over to the side of the road, breathing deeply. The pain slowly receded, but a revelation hit him. His entire approach to unlocking value was flawed. Something had to change. He knew it would not be comfortable.

Story 2: Collaboration and seeking synergy

Terry had just returned from a refreshing year-end break and had spent some time considering how Impact Inc. could unlock greater value from the business. Competitive forces had placed increased pressure on all their operations, and the impact was being felt on margins. His key reflection was that the organisation needed to double down on collaboration and seek greater synergies. To win in the market, they needed to work smartly, collaborate more, drive radical simplicity, and remove wasted executive time on internal matters.

Rather than wait for a formal meeting, Terry called for an executive brainstorming session. He outlined his thinking on greater collaboration, synergy, and value unlocking. Terry stressed the importance of creating psychological safety for the discussion, so that the best thinking could surface. Like any sports team winning a World Cup, unless we work together, we cannot win. We must work together to find synergies and unlock value opportunities. He looked around the room, "This is our collective team effort, so I am comfortable knowing each of you will put the organisation first." There was universal acceptance, as reflected in nods of approval.

Priya, the human capital executive, raised her hand. "Before we proceed, could I suggest that we divide into two teams for this session? For each idea or collaborative opportunity, we have one team pushing the art of the possible and pushing the boundaries, and the second team seeking to find synergy and improvements from an overall view." Everyone agreed on the way the workshop would be run.

Terry continued, "I am also aware we may have metrics or key performance indicators that contradict our collaborative efforts. Rest assured, Thabo and I will review those and ensure alignment. One more thing, I encourage you to please identify and remove any obstacles or barriers that will limit our teams from working together. The Executive Team spent the rest of the session brainstorming ideas and opportunities. By the end of the session, there was a positive energy, which had heartened the leadership team.

Over the next quarter, Terry kept close to the business and stimulated collaboration and synergy across the organisation, reminding everyone they were part of a winning team. It was encouraging to observe how executives worked seamlessly together, how teams challenged each other positively, how new ways of working were embedded, how radical simplicity was a mantra, and how everyone embraced profitable value creation. Thabo, the financial executive, had also radically simplified the internal cost allocations, which previously had been a source of frustration across the business. The business was set up for success.

Another positive development from Priya, the human resources executive, was the advent of cross-functional teams. These had been established to solve complex business challenges, drive innovation, generate opportunities, or shape business solutions. These networked teams became an entrenched way of working, ensuring that collaboration trumped internal silos. Once team members had seen the power of collective effort, there was no going back.

Terry and Thabo reviewed the financial results before the half-year review session. Many indicators showed positive trends, and the overall business results were pleasing. Collaboration at an organisational level had proved to be the correct strategy. They agreed on a few areas to focus on, where they felt there was further opportunity for margin growth or removal of wasted overheads.

The Executive Team met off-site in a positive frame of mind. Terry started the session by congratulating the team on the collective effort, "The results of your collaboration have unlocked synergy and enhanced business value. Job well done, team." It was evident from the smiles around the conference room that each leader was equally pleased with the collective outcome achieved thus far.

Terry then asked each executive to share their success stories of collaboration and in seeking synergy. The sharing of success stories took well over two hours and magically was a catalyst for the positive vibe in the room and across the entire organisation. The team shared many examples, including: driving simplicity, removing waste, connecting the dots, asking open-ended questions, innovative ideas from unexpected people, and collective team efforts. However, what stood out for everyone was what it had done for the culture of Impact Inc. Terry was quick to flag this. "Team, the energy your collaborative efforts have unleashed in our people excites me more than any value-unlocking examples shared. This energy will differentiate us for years to come. I'm excited about what the future holds."

As Terry drove home after the Executive Team workshop, he was confident that the future looked positive and that the foundations for winning their World Cup were solid. He will sleep well tonight.

PART D

ORGANISATION

Mindset shift 19: Cumbersome and reactive ➡ Future-focussed agility

Mindset shift 20: Compliant, tick-the-box ➡ Focus energy on outcomes

Mindset shift 21: Inward-focussed ➡ Customer-centric

Mindset shift 22: Apathy and bystanders ➡ Commitment to decisions

Mindset shift 23: Excuses and passing blame ➡ Responsible, accountable, and ownership

Mindset shift 24: Mediocrity and complexity ➡ Excellence and simplicity

MINDSET SHIFT 19

Cumbersome and reactive ➝ Future-focussed agility

Question: Does your organisation respond to trends proactively and with agility?

Key mindset transition: Shifting from being cumbersome to organisational agility.

👀 Observations

	Cumbersome and reactive	Future-focussed agility
Expressions (what we hear)	• That will never happen to us. • We have lots of time to reply and make a call. • Lengthy and fact-free debates.	• Future seen as exciting. • Encourage people and provide opportunities to learn. • Seeking a faster, more effective or smarter way.
Behaviours (what we see and feel)	• Slow decision making. • Absence of a plan or options. • Fear of the future and what is new.	• Empowerment and enablement. • Responsive, proactive & agile. • Focus on strengths.
Ways of working (what we experience)	• Risk mitigation is weak. • Relevance bias to the information at hand. • Fear of the future.	• Learn from mistakes & move on. • Confidence in the future. • Identify and develop future capabilities.

🔑 Key message

Creating an environment where curiosity, innovation, experiential learning, and organisational agility thrive requires an intentional effort.

Future-focussed agility means the organisation is flexible, learns rapidly, makes quick decisions and can swiftly respond to changes in markets or customer demands. Agile organisations can adapt their ways of working to respond quickly and capitalise on market opportunities.

On the contrary, you have cumbersome organisations that are reactive in responding to a crisis. They ignore obvious trends and miss obvious opportunities. These organisations often think they have all the answers internally and take their time to adapt to shifting market trends.

Future-focussed agility only happens by design and requires leaders to go first. Designing an agile organisation requires a focus on multiple factors, but leadership behaviours and ways of working are among the most critical. Leaders set the tone for future-focussed agility and actively lead a learning culture. It is difficult for an organisation to be agile if the leaders do not demonstrate this mindset.

For agility to flourish, it requires an enabling environment. This includes reviewing the rules of engagement, operating model, calibre of people, employee experience and business processes. A disenabling environment creates obstacles, frustration, and barriers, which fundamentally stifles people.

One of the cornerstones of agility is learning, failing fast, and being intentional in using mistakes as teachable moments. After all, we often learn the most from mistakes. Many organisations are built on years of processes that create inefficiencies and limit the ability to make rapid changes. These organisations inadvertently cultivate complexity, reducing the ability to stay proactive and relevant to their customers.

Organisational agility has a few key principles. These could include: focus on growth, customer-centric, responsive, adaptable, innovative, collaborative, integrated, effectiveness, simplicity and role clarity. Agility is not just a mindset but also an operating model structuring choice.

Often, what holds us back is the things that we should stop doing. Daniel Goleman[18] asks a key question: "What will you say 'no' to in order to create the time you need for working on the goal?"

👣 Practical steps

Possible considerations to drive future-focussed agility

- Use mistakes as teachable moments.
- Encourage curiosity and seeking out new perspectives.
- Support innovation and future-focussed thinking.
- Drive experiential learning and a learning culture.
- Remove obstacles and barriers to organisational agility.

ⓘ Warning signals that a shift is required

- Mistakes are punished.
- Failure is not tolerated.
- Reactive to issues or events.
- Learning is not encouraged.
- Obsession with analysing what went wrong.

📖 Anecdotal business examples

I have observed many organisations become increasingly cumbersome, reactive, bureaucratic, bogged down in detail, and mired in complexity. This is often more prevalent in larger organisations, which become increasingly complex over time. As the business grows, more processes, systems and governance are added to counter an increasingly complex world. Sadly, though, very few dedicate time and energy to removing unwanted complexity, often because the pace of business becomes increasingly frenetic. Linked to this complexity is initiative overload, especially when things are going well. These emanate from corporate head offices, which believe the initiatives are value-adding. However, as organisations go through fluctuating business cycles, few leaders step back and see what can be stopped. So, the workload and complexity increase. I refer to this as cultivating complexity versus driving radical simplicity.

I have spent many years in management consulting, in addition to my time in industry. The larger management consulting businesses are becoming increasingly complex and hampered by governance and compliance issues. Whilst some of this is required, it is apparent that this makes the larger organisations bulky and cumbersome. Josh Bersin also covered this topic in his book Irresistible.[19] Over the last few years, I have worked at a small boutique consultancy where agility is prevalent. This agility is good for clients, and it fosters an exciting culture. By way of example, in some of the larger consulting firms, it can take longer than two weeks to respond to client requests. We recently responded to a complex enquiry in less than twenty-four hours. Where would you rather be?

Business issue for the two stories: Organisational agility

Reminder: As explained in the introduction, the two stories are told as opposite extremes of the mindset transition. Leaders should understand the tensions between the two extremes and find a balance that best fits their context or situation.

Story 1: Cumbersome and reactive

Brash Inc. had been secure in certain market segments for years, and with a stable customer base, it was not surprising that Storm felt comfortable with the status quo. Given the long-standing customer relationships, he felt very confident that they would be lifelong customers if they delivered consistent quality, on time. He was also pressuring his sales executives to increase prices, as some market segments were a clear cash cow for the organisation.

During a recent sales and marketing meeting, a new sales manager flagged changing trends in customer needs, the use of technology by smaller start-ups, shifting demand patterns, and declining prices in other markets. Storm listened, somewhat amused by the naivety of the young manager. He was about to launch a sarcastic comment when he noticed that some of his senior management team nodded at the sales manager as he spoke about the trends. Wanting to maintain the upper hand, he remarked, "Thanks for that, but it will never happen to us, at least not in the next few years. Let's stay focussed on what has worked well for us. As they say, *Never fix what is not broken.*" The glances he received indicated different views, but he chose to ignore them.

Storm walked past the sales executive and enquired about the price increases they had discussed. The response was muted: "Yes, we have implemented the price increases, but many customers are unhappy."

Storm replied, "They always say that. Just keep the prices up. Besides, where else could they go?" The sales executive shrugged his shoulders and dashed for the coffee machine.

A few weeks later, Storm received a report reflecting the loss of a key customer. The customer's CEO was also a long-standing friend and golf partner. Feeling irate, he called the CEO, "Hey Fred, I see we have lost you as a customer? Why? We go back many years. You can't do this to me."

The CEO replied, "Hey Storm, I know we go back a long way, but quite frankly, some suppliers are using new technology which suits us better. Besides the technology, it is cheaper, and they are contributing to our overall solution design. We don't have a choice."

Storm replied, "OK, thanks, Fred. I'm sure they won't last long in the market. I value your business, so I will hold our prices and give you a ten per cent volume discount. Let me know if that will change your mind." When the call ended, he stared out of the window, frustrated, believing that Fred and his company would come to their senses.

As the weeks passed, Storm received increasing feedback on key shifts in the market and how the price increase strategy had backfired. To retain customers, they had to decrease prices, but even this proved to have a limited impact. Anxious about what was happening, Storm called for another sales and marketing meeting to assess the status and agree on corrective actions. Unable to control his anxiety and anger, he blurted out, "Can someone please tell me what on earth is happening and why we can't fix our sales?" The room went quiet. "Anybody?"

After an eerie silence in which you could hear a pin drop, the sales executive responded, "We should have listened to our sales manager a few months ago. He provides us with insights into the technology trends. We have been too slow to respond and have probably lost more than half of our sales in three market segments. The changes are unthinkable; we could never have anticipated it." He glanced nervously around the room, hoping someone would say something to alleviate the painful moment.

Storm was visibly rattled by this revelation. "I suppose you are right. It is a black swan event. Nobody could have seen it coming."

The young sales manager was about to say something, but the sales executive next to him cautioned him to remain silent. This was not the time to annoy Storm any further. The sales executive meekly replied, "I suppose we should learn from this, so we don't make the same mistake in the future."

Storm loudly stated, "You bet. For all your sakes, I hope we never make this mistake again." He remained seated after everyone else had left the room. He held his head in his hands and muttered to himself, "Maybe I could have done something. I am probably afraid to make the changes needed." As he mulled this over, he also regretted his behaviour and how he had spoken to his colleagues and team. He finally left the room, frustrated in many ways, realising he needed to offer apologies and change his ways. He had contributed to the decline, and this left him with a numb feeling.

Story 2: Future-focussed agility

Impact Inc. has been successful in certain market segments for years and has had a stable customer base. Even though they had long-standing customer relationships, maintained consistent quality, and delivered on time, Terry and the leadership team felt that those customers would not always be lifelong customers, and they sensed that key market shifts were brewing. Whilst there was a tendency to push prices up in market segments that were a cash cow for the organisation, they knew that the market trends indicated otherwise.

During a recent sales and marketing meeting, a newly promoted sales manager was quite animated in sharing changing trends in customer needs, the use of technology by smaller start-ups, shifting demand patterns, and declining prices in global markets. Terry listened intently, realising that much of what was being said resonated with him and aligned with his intuitive thoughts on the key trends in the selected market segments. He was suitably impressed by the young manager. "Well done. Those are great insights. As an organisation, we must be agile and future-ready to meet customer needs." He paused before asking, "Any thoughts on how we might respond to the shifting trends?"

One of his Executive Team replied, "We have been working with production, technology providers, and a customer working group in anticipation of the new technology. Whilst we are only at a prototype stage, I sense we need to accelerate the refinement, usage and adoption of the new technology, both internally and with our customers."

Terry invited the meeting to further dialogue, and collectively they agreed to accelerate technology development and avoid being caught by surprise in the future. They also discussed a revised pricing strategy and debated ideas for additional value-adding services, which would continue to make their market offering attractive to customers.

After mulling over the sales meeting, Terry directly engaged five of their largest customers, some of whom had become close personal friends after years of doing business together. His message to each was clear and consistent: our customers are important to us, we recognise the changes in needs, we are working on newer enabling technology, and we want to co-create a viable product. The response was overwhelmingly positive, and all except one customer committed to trial the new technology and how the product offering would work out.

Only one customer was non-committal, stating, "Look, Terry, I value our business relationship, but I am giving this new start-up an opportunity. I must demonstrate to the rest of my team that we are future-focussed and willing to innovate and experiment. I am sure you understand." Terry nodded, aware that he probably should do the same.

As the weeks flew by, Terry kept close to the technology development, his core team and their customers. Positive signals were surfacing, and green shoots were emerging from customer interactions. Other than one, they had retained most key customers and only made small margin sacrifices.

Terry looked up as he heard the knock at his door and ushered in his sales executive. The executive beamed, "I have good news. We are ready to launch the new technology six weeks ahead of schedule. I want to call a sales and marketing meeting to discuss our launch to customers."

Terry smiled, "Well done to you and the teams. Please send my congratulations. I'm happy to call the meeting immediately."

Terry opened the meeting and asked everyone to give a round of applause for a great collective effort. He handed over to the sales executive to take them through the meeting. He shared the overall progress, gave broad recognition and praised the team for their future-focussed agility and resilience.

Terry asked, "What is the team's thinking on pricing?"

The sales executive replied, "We anticipate that the overall price will come down by fifteen per cent, but importantly, our margin in absolute terms shows a slight improvement because of the savings created by the technology. Indications from our customers are highly positive, and it is unlikely that any of them will switch. Our proactive approach and organisational agility have kept us on the front foot."

Another executive added, "Another important spin-off is that one of the start-ups has approached us and entered into a long-term collaboration agreement. A great outcome all round."

Terry remained seated after his team left the room. He was proud of his team and felt privileged to lead such a dynamic team. He also realised that as the leader, he needed to continually remain agile and demonstrate it with the tone from the top.

MINDSET SHIFT 20

Compliant, tick the box ➜ Focus energy on outcomes

Question: Is your organisation focussed on what really matters and driving sustainable outcomes?

Key mindset transition: Shifting from compliance, ticking the box and risk-averse to focussing energy on sustainable outcomes.

👀 Observations

	Compliant, tick the box	Focus energy on outcomes
Expressions (what we hear)	• Have you ticked all the boxes? • As long as it makes the auditors happy. • I'm following instructions.	• Will this drive the desired outcome. • What will move us forward. • Challenge conventional wisdom.
Behaviours (what we see and feel)	• Seeking weakness and flaws in ideas. • Justifying a decision, regardless of obvious trends. • Argue against common sense.	• Show recognition for effort. • Recognise outputs. • Encourage results.
Ways of working (what we experience)	• Lost in the details and miss the big idea. • Process hampers simplicity or defies logic. • Use excuses to protect yourself.	• Drive effective outcomes. • Honest two-way feedback. • Engage for a collective outcome.

🗝 Key message

Driving sustainable outcomes means leaders understand what really matters, have clarity on what the right things are to do, can explain why they are doing them well and focus their energy on those things. That may be quite a mouthful when you say it, but it is essential for driving outcomes, which unlock sustainable value. The other extreme is where the entire organisation's energy is focussed on being compliant and ticking the box. This is not stimulating and is unlikely to generate sustainable outcomes or value.

I often ask leaders the question, "What really matters?". They stare at me until I ask the question again, "What really matters?" For many leaders and teams, there could be dozens, if not hundreds, of things that must get done. You cannot do one hundred things well. Simple maths is that if you had one hundred priorities and you have a forty-hour week, you only have twenty-four minutes per priority, per week. Hence, the important task for leaders is to understand what really matters for the greatest impact. I think you should not have over five super-priorities at a time, which should receive approximately half of your time allocation.

Once you have clarity on what really matters, you should be clear about what the right things are that need to be executed.

- Have you done the strategic thinking?
- Do you know how to lead the change?
- Are you clear on how to enable execution?

These questions may seem trivial, but most leaders I engage with struggle to articulate the things that drive effective strategy execution. This is often because they feel it is intuitive or obvious, but cannot articulate it. Quite frankly, it is useless unless it can be explained and others can execute on it.

To truly drive improved execution, it is vital that you can explain why you are doing things well and what great looks like. Otherwise, any result or outcome will do. When the above three aspects are clear, it is easier to infuse energy, which will deliver outcomes or value.

When organisations are compliance-focussed and ticking the box, they likely drain energy and are unlikely to achieve the desired outcomes. I also observe that in these circumstances, the employees get sucked into the detail and completely miss the big picture. One of my favourite questions in this situation is, "Is it directionally correct or precisely wrong?"

A good example of this mindset shift is Shell's Goal Zero initiative[20] aimed at improving safety. The initiative was primarily a departure from procedural compliance to creating psychological safety, allowing everyone to challenge safety-related risks.

Practical steps

High-level steps that drive a focus on outcomes and sustainable results

- Understand what really matters, which will drive desired outcomes.
- Do strategic thinking to articulate what you are solving for and what great would look like.
- Understand why this is important and lead the change to unlock discretionary energy.
- Remove obstacles and create psychological safety for people to challenge.
- Create an enabling environment for effective execution.

Warning signals that a shift is required

- Compliance requirements outweigh common sense.
- Processes are increasingly complex.
- The volume of work to meet obligations bears no relation to the revenue-generating work.
- The administrative burden cultivates complexity.
- People focus on so many details that they miss the big opportunities.

Anecdotal business examples

A typical business example frequently observed relates to the execution of capital projects. The contrast between compliance and outcomes is often prevalent. Whilst compliance is important, ticking the box should not come at the expense of the capital project outcomes. Closely linked to this juxtaposition is the critical issue of the primary project driver, namely, cost, quality or time. These three drivers often generate fierce debate. It may seem trivial, but driving one at the expense of another can severely impact the desired outcomes. However, I believe the most important value driver is whether the capital project will be ready to deliver revenue as planned. This value driver is often way more value accretive.

Another key business challenge is the growing compliance, regulatory, and governance requirements, which are pervasive and increasing at astonishing rates. Most people and organisations can't cope with the volume of work required to meet these onerous obligations. Also concerning is the increasing tendency to pass the burden from Boards to Executive Teams and finally onto managers. Whilst important, the onus is on leadership teams and corporate offices to rethink compliance, make it palatable from a volume and understanding point of view, and drive outcomes for the most critical elements. In one discussion with a multi-national, we debated an onerous thousand-page-plus report, which was challenging to read, let alone understand. I challenged the team to identify the ten things people must do right. Once this landed, it reduced compliance risk by a substantial percentage.

Business issue for the two stories: Mega projects

Reminder: As explained in the introduction, the two stories are told as opposite extremes of the mindset transition. Leaders should understand the tensions between the two extremes and find a balance that best fits their context or situation.

Story 1: Compliant tick the box

Storm was preparing for an investor presentation of their new mega project. The scale of the capital project dwarfed anything that Brash Inc. had undertaken in its history. The project value would double the invested capital and boost their revenue by more than double. It was a big deal for Brash Inc. This was a personal flagship project for Storm, which would set him up for success in his final few years with the organisation. While some challenged him that it was an ego project, he consistently replied that it was laying a sustainable legacy for the future.

The project was scheduled to be completed over four years, for one billion dollars. From Storm's perspective, two key project drivers were important: the completion date would coincide with his thirty-year tenure, and the cost was a personal assurance he had given the Board before the project commenced. In his interactions with the project director, he emphasised that the date and the cost were non-negotiable. He had already replaced one project director who did not readily agree to these parameters.

Midway through, Storm received the project status report from the project director, which ran into many pages of analysis, reports, s-curves and figures. Storm felt overwhelmed by the volume and complexity of the report, but took solace from the new project director, who had come through the operational ranks. He seemed confident that everything was on track. Storm requested a project steering committee meeting to review the presentation on the mega project. The project director shared the presentation with such confidence that it was hard for anyone to contemplate that the project was facing any issues. Storm felt some unease, but figured it was merely his anxiety.

The conference room was packed on the day of the investor presentation. Storm again realised the importance of the mega project and what it meant for Brash Inc. and its investors. Storm welcomed everyone and initiated the presentation with a general overview of the project and its criticality in meeting Brash Inc.'s strategic objectives over the coming few years. He wrapped up his introduction, feeling pleased, and asked the project director to share a more detailed presentation on the project. Storm noted some unease amongst the investors and some funders, and was caught completely off guard when the investors started pummelling them with questions about the project. The questions challenged key assumptions, timelines, completion date, project leadership, key risks, cash flows, variations, supplier contracts and poor collaboration between the professional teams.

The project director responded somewhat aggressively to many of the questions and challenged some questions with a level of sarcasm. This implied that the investors were clueless about the mega project and that he was in control. One investor plugged away with questions and created doubt for others present when he persisted and demonstrated that the responses did not align. The investor concluded, "I hear the answers, but mark my words, this project will fail to meet schedule and cost milestones." Furious, Storm closed the session and avoided engaging with anyone directly.

On his way home, the Chair called him, "Storm, given how the investor presentation ended, we have no option but to call for third-party assurance." Reluctantly, Storm agreed.

Storm engaged an external audit firm that had always been friendly towards Brash Inc., although it had never been its auditors. Storm's brief to them left little doubt about the outcomes expected in the report. It had to demonstrate that the project was on track to meet the initial business case.

In the interim, Storm visited the project himself and was surprised by the scale and number of people on site. However, he had a hollow feeling that the construction was not where it should be and found it hard to imagine how the project would be completed on time. As they went around the site, Storm asked questions of the team, but the project director always responded, continually emphasising that everything was on track. Soon after the visit, an assurance report was issued showing that the project was fully compliant from a process point of view. The report indicated some concerns, but was phrased in such a way that it appeared to indicate all was well. Storm was convinced that if everyone followed the processes, the outcomes should be satisfactory.

As Storm approached his thirtieth year with Brash Inc., it became clear that the completion milestone would be missed by several months, if not a year. Additionally, the Board had requested a completely independent assurance report. When he received the approved copy, it was clear that the capital cost would be exceeded by at least fifty per cent. It was an unequivocal disaster in his view. The final line of the executive summary said it all: *poor project management has led to a poor outcome, despite the processes that were followed.*

Storm felt his heart beating, aware that he had ignored many signals and lessons related to mega projects. His personal bias had caused him to lose focus on the real project drivers and their implications. His ego had blindsided him.

Story 2: Focus energy on outcomes

Terry was preparing for an investor presentation about their new mega project. Although Impact Inc. had undertaken large projects before, this project was significantly bigger than any previously undertaken. Collectively, the Board and management team agreed to scale back the initial size of the project. Wisely, they had taken on a project that was more manageable and within their overall risk tolerance. Everyone in the organisation realised that this project was critical for the long-term sustainability of the business, and hence it became collectively owned as a mega project.

When the mega project was approved, it was agreed that the primary driver should be an asset enabling revenue to be delivered from day one. The detailed feasibility and design had been approved, and an adequate schedule and cost contingency buffer had been built in. Initially, when the mega project was mooted, there was intense pressure to appoint an internal operational candidate. Terry and the Chair had resisted this temptation, appointing a highly regarded project director who was experienced in delivering a project of this kind and had a proven track record. Terry understood that the right project leader was critical to success.

Leading up to the investor presentation, Terry and his Executive Team acquainted themselves with the project and reviewed the wide-ranging report. In a pre-meeting, Terry requested that the project director take them through the details. His experience was instantly felt, and he articulated the project complexity into comprehensible information, ensuring that everyone was clear on the real project status. The project director was also key in highlighting an important supplier risk that could impact the project, but gave comfort that the contingency was adequate to deal with the eventuality.

On the day of the investor presentation, the conference room was packed with people. This reminded Terry of the mega project's importance to the sustainable future of Impact Inc. It was a significant project in many respects. Terry welcomed everyone present and handed over to the project director, who meticulously took the investors through the project's complexity in a practical and relatable way. He ended the presentation with drone footage, fed live from the project site. Terry noted the level of comfort among the investors who appreciated the detail and authentic style of the project director. Investors probed several questions, but you could sense they were comfortable with the clear and intuitive responses.

On his way home after the investor presentation, the Chair called, "Well done to you and the team, Terry. It certainly seems as if things are well on track with the project. Notwithstanding, I was requested to conduct a third-party assurance exercise to comply with good practice." Terry immediately agreed, as he was comfortable that things were on track.

Terry and some of his Executive Team conducted their usual site visit to experience the project progress firsthand. Overall, Terry felt a sense of comfort, but in one area of the project, it was evident that it was lagging. Terry asked one of the construction managers to explain why this area was lagging. He replied, "We had a few senior team members among the professional team and ourselves who were not aligned. We have engaged everyone and established a new rhythm for ways of working. Based on the alignment, we should reduce the lag." Terry was surprised by the openness but soon realised that it aligned with their corporate culture.

Soon after this visit, the Chair shared a third-party assurance report with Terry and the project team. The focus was on the project outcomes rather than getting overly bogged down in process and compliance detail. The key benefit was that they had identified a critical item that could have impacted the overall schedule. Fortunately, the findings and recommendations gave Impact Inc. ample time to rectify the deficiency. The project team responded maturely and hastily rectified the issue.

As the project neared completion, it was clear that the mega project was on track to deliver revenue from day one as planned. On the positive side, although some of the schedule float had been absorbed, the overall contingency was only partially spent. The project would therefore be delivered on time, under budget and enable operations as planned. Terry congratulated the team, "Well done on a very successful mega project execution."

MINDSET SHIFT 21

Inward focussed → Customer-centric

Question: Is your organisation focussed on driving a positive customer experience?

Key mindset transition: Shifting from inward-focussed and endless meetings to customer-centric and focussed on the customer experience.

👀 Observations

	Inward focussed	Customer-centric
Expressions (what we hear)	• Internally absorbed and focussed. • Protocols and processes that don't make sense. • Frustration with customers.	• Customer experience. • How can we better serve the customer? • Focus on customer needs.
Behaviours (what we see and feel)	• Change resistant. • Don't know what customer values or needs. • Protection of silo or business unit.	• Positive customer experience and engagement. • Engaging and serving. • Keeping promises.
Ways of working (what we experience)	• Excess governance. • Cumbersome processes & procedures. • Internal silos hamper effectiveness.	• Simplify how customers can engage with us. • External customer experience. • Processes developed with the customer in mind.

🔑 Key message

Being customer-centric means that your entire organisation is focussed on the customer, client or consumer. For almost any commercially driven business, without customers, there is no revenue and probably no business. Despite the importance of the customer, it remains a fact that many organisations allow themselves to become extremely inwardly focussed. Therefore, every leader and employee should be focussed on the customers' needs and their experience of your organisation.

Customer experience entails linking all efforts throughout the value chain to ensure that it delivers a positive experience when a customer interacts with any part of your organisation, whether directly or indirectly. The customer experience includes: interaction with your brand, products, levels of service, their experience of engaging your employees, value for money and durability of what you have sold or delivered. Customers have growing options, so your organisation should prioritise efforts to ensure you are the provider of choice. A quote from Jeff Bezos puts a different lens on it: "We see our customers as invited guests to a party, and we are hosts. It's our job every day to make every important aspect of the customer experience a little better."

The acid test of a customer-centric organisation is when all your employees can articulate the customer experience and their role in it. More importantly, your customers should be able to explain their customer experience and share this with others. This implies that customers can clearly articulate how their needs are met and how their expectations are fulfilled.

Being customer-centric also means that every process in an organisation should have a tangible link to the customer experience. If any effort or process does not add value to the customer or is overly internally focussed, then it should be flagged for review. This implies that every employee can articulate how they contribute to delivering a positive customer experience. It remains intriguing how many people, processes or activities in an organisation have no clear link to customer needs.

A great example of the customer-centric mindset is Southwest Airlines. They often come up in leadership case studies. In Harvard[21] case studies, they talk of "end-to-end ownership of the customer experience." This implies a deliberate breaking down of internal silos to work together, and thereby drive an effective customer experience.

👣 Practical steps

Considerations in becoming more customer-centric

- Engage customers to ensure we constantly get an external view of customer needs.
- Define customer experience and how it will meet customer expectations.
- Ensure that your organisation is constantly seeking to improve customer experience.
- Ensure that all internal ways of working, processes and systems serve the customer experience and make it easy to do business with us.
- Ensure that all employees understand their role in delivering on the customer experience.

❗ Warning signals that a shift is required

- Internal projects and focus dominate organisational efforts and energy.
- Your customer experience is not codified to deliver it consistently.
- Employees are unable to link their efforts to how it impacts the customer experience.
- Your revenue is under pressure or declining.
- Customers find it difficult to work with you.

📖 Anecdotal business examples

Sadly, an inward focus is pervasive in many organisations. There are many reasons, including: market pressure, increasing governance, increasingly complex processes, misaligned ways of working, headcount reductions and the fickle needs and expectations of increasingly diverse customers. This is often compounded by increasing demands from shareholders for better returns. This melting pot of complexity can push the customer, their needs, expectations and the customer experience to the back of the priority queue. The result is predictable: without customers who have a positive experience of your organisation, they will simply vote with their wallets and go elsewhere.

I work in a management consulting organisation, and our business is fundamentally about our clients. Our ability to remain sustainable highly depends on a positive client experience, from the moment they engage us until we have completed a deliverable or a project. Every moment is crucial, either adding positively to the experience or detracting from it. Probably most critical are interpersonal relationships, which create a human bond. Following any initial engagement, there needs to be a consistent experience of the project, including surprising the client on the upside. The value of a positive client experience will drive trust and referrals.

Business issue for the two stories: Customer experience

Reminder: As explained in the introduction, the two stories are told as opposite extremes of the mindset transition. Leaders should understand the tensions between the two extremes and find a balance that best fits their context or situation.

Story 1: Inward focussed

Storm stared at the sales report for the last year. It was evident that Brash Inc. had a challenge around customer retention. Anchor customers, who had been around for years had disappeared from the client sales report. As far as Storm was concerned, it was both a sales and marketing failure. How else could they be losing customers at such a rapid rate? As he mulled over the report, it was clear that they needed to look internally and dig deep to find the root cause of the issue. His recent requests for answers from both sales and marketing were unconvincing.

Once again, he summoned the sales and marketing directors and their direct reports to a full-day workshop to understand the challenge. He expected that debating the issue would give them a different outcome. As usual, the day started with a detailed variance analysis and a multitude of defensive responses about why the market was where it was. The ramblings about changing customer needs, costly distribution, packaging that didn't work and poor service delivery were pervasive in the morning session. It certainly painted a gloomy picture. The afternoon session sought to identify root causes. Rather than having an honest dialogue about customer needs and root causes, the focus was on the cost reduction of key employees and the energy-sapping internal meetings. The day ended with no conclusive answers, commitments or actions.

Storm was furious as he reflected on the wholly unsatisfactory workshop, which was inward-focussed and not insightful. Irritated, he crafted an email that sent a tough message giving instructions for frequent deep dive meetings to understand the issues and find meaningful solutions. When he mentioned the issue over a weekend lunch, one of his family members sarcastically stated that Brash Inc. should be more in touch with its customers. Inwardly, he was outraged, but he realised that this was true. He quietly grunted an acknowledgement.

On Monday morning, Storm followed up on his previous emails, instructing them to do customer surveys to gain a better understanding of their needs and concerns. This email was followed by a request to meet with the sales director. On Tuesday, they met to discuss the situation, and the sales director boldly responded to Storm, "Quite frankly, Storm, the way we are going about customer retention is wrong. Lengthy internal meetings and surveys will not help us turn things around. I need people to visit customers and truly understand their needs. However, to do this, I need people, and of course, the last round of head count cuts saw us lose the very team we need right now." Storm could feel the tension in the room, but realised that the situation was the reality of short-sighted decisions. They mulled it over and agreed to engage a team of temporary external contractors.

Within weeks, it became evident that Brash Inc. had missed many vital signs regarding the health of customer relationships and needs. The feedback was clear that Brash Inc. had fallen behind and customers were leaving for other suppliers who met their needs, were more innovative and provided a more meaningful customer experience.

Storm realised that the leadership of the business had failed their customers and employees. Employees were disempowered to make a difference to the customer experience. The sales and marketing director led the next working session and, for the first time, allowed an honest conversation. The response was brutally honest, but tough. The teams realised that a lot of work was needed to remedy past practises and then turn them around. Storm had participated but was in the background. He painfully realised that the sales numbers would take months to improve. The inward focus and wasted internal efforts had been value-destroying.

Storm and the management team were forced to revise the business forecasts and advise the Board and market. Reactions were harsh, and many critics felt justified in their harsh criticism. Storm found it difficult not to be defensive and respond, but realised that this was one of those moments in his career where he had to suck it up. It certainly did not feel good, but he realised he had played a leadership role in getting the organisation here.

Following some reflective time, he called in some of the leadership team to convey a simple message, "We need to become customer-centric with immediate effect." He also offered a rare apology for his leadership deficiency. He hoped it was not too late.

Story 2: Customer-centric

Terry analysed the sales reports for the last year and noted the sagging trends in customer retention. He was aware of new competitors in the market, and rather than blaming sales and marketing, he realised that Impact Inc. had a business challenge. It required bold leadership to rectify the situation. Tempted to look inward, Terry quickly realised that the answers lay externally with their customers and how their organisation responded to changing needs. Previous internally focussed workshops had provided limited market traction.

In collaboration with the sales and marketing directors, Terry set up a half-day brainstorming workshop to explore customer retention, needs and customer experience. Rather than blame and analyse historical data, they allowed the teams to have frank discussions about root causes and what Brash Inc. could do differently. They quickly moved past some of the usual excuses and started having forthright debates about what needed to change to drive a step change in customer experience. Although the session ended without clear answers, the team committed to actions that would hopefully produce positive results.

Terry realised that the half-day workshop would not change the trends overnight, but he was encouraged by the positive attitude of team members, despite tough circumstances. Over a weekend lunch, the topic of customer experience came up. One family member spoke up, indicating that most organisations had lost touch with the customer, adding that their friends felt the same way about Impact Inc. Terry was caught off-guard by the statement, but replied, "Thank you for that honesty, I did not realise that. I will investigate it as a matter of urgency." Conversation quickly drifted to a major football final being played that evening.

On Monday, Terry reached out to the sales director and called for a meeting. Terry added they needed to engage their top customers and understand where Impact Inc had missed the mark on customer experience. It was important to obtain their perspective and feedback, rather than assume what they might be thinking.

On Tuesday, they met to deliberate the situation, and the sales director started the discussion, "I have considered your comment from yesterday. You are right. We have been thinking incorrectly about the customer experience. Without realising it, we have become inwardly focussed. We need to visit customers and truly understand their needs and expectations. We also need to understand their views of how they experience us. However, I need more people despite the recent headcount freeze."

Terry acknowledged how the headcount freeze had affected them and agreed to provide the resources to improve the customer experience and, hopefully, sales. It was vital to make the correct long-term decision and not be trapped by short-term cost-reduction pressures.

The team prioritised engaging customers and all other stakeholders in the value chain to understand the customer experience, how this met expectations and what Impact Inc. needed to do differently. The most important realisation for the sales director was that customers felt ignored. Although difficult to absorb, it was a major revelation. Customer feedback from multiple engagements gave Terry and Impact Inc. a clear understanding of how they had missed key signals and, bluntly, where they had disappointed customers. The toughest feedback to acknowledge was that customers were increasingly finding it difficult to work with

Impact Inc. because of the excessive steps in the sales process and the sluggish response to service requests.

After a few weeks, the sales director reported back to Terry and indicated that his team had internalised much of the customer feedback and were taking positive actions, which would remedy the untenable customer experience situation. He also advised that they had launched a campaign to remove any obstacles in the way of working or processes that did not add value to either products or the service they delivered to the customer. Early indications were that customers were returning. There was work to be done, but the green shoots of sales growth were coming through. Terry thanked the sales director and his team for their efforts.

Although the quarterly report to the Board would be difficult, he was comforted by the knowledge that the organisation would do its best to turn things around. He also reflected on his role in missing the sales trends and vowed to dedicate more strategic thinking to this matter in the future. He reminded himself of an adage that the customer was king. Thankfully, they had reacted timeously.

MINDSET SHIFT 22

Apathy and bystanders ➜ Commitment to decisions

Question: Is your culture conducive to effective decision making?

Key mindset transition: Shifting from apathy, fact-free debates and bystanders to full commitment to decisions and following through.

👀 Observations

	Apathy and bystanders	Commitment to decisions
Expressions (what we hear)	• Defensiveness and blame culture. • It wasn't my decision. • I don't care what they decide.	• Are there other views we need? • Despite differences, are we aligned? • We're committed and stand by the decision.
Behaviours (what we see and feel)	• Stick to their opinion. • Cynicism and negativity. • Silence and poor body language.	• Asking clarifying questions in the meeting. • Consider all views, then align. • Commit to and accept decisions.
Ways of working (what we experience)	• Biassed assumptions. • Loud voices overrule experts. • Decisions are illogical and are biassed by hierarchy.	• Assumptions tested & validated. • Intuitive decisions tested for value. • Robust decision-making process.

🔑 Key message

Commitment to decisions made by both leaders and employees is fundamental to building trust and enabling execution effectiveness. Naturally, when leaders engage in a robust dialogue on a topic, there may be differences of opinion. All voices or perspectives need to be surfaced before common ground is established. Once this is done, a final decision must be made. What then follows is of paramount importance. Once a decision is made, everyone involved must accept and commit to that decision. Failure to commit is likely to destroy trust and risk decision failure.

Commitment is enhanced when everyone understands why the decision is important and how they can relate to it. This makes it easier to commit to a decision rather than forcing it. This does not preclude robust debate to ensure the correct decision is made. Commitment is the act of dedicating yourself to a decision or task and then staying the course. The organisation will experience commitment to a decision when all leaders are aligned, think similarly, say the same thing and act in accordance.

Commitment entails key elements, such as a robust decision-making process (explained in practical steps) and embracing the agreed-upon decision or course of action. It also requires clear communication, ownership, accountability, someone taking action and importantly, following through to ensure the decision or action is executed effectively.

A lack of commitment often leads to distrust, organisational waste, silos, internal dissent, and poor execution. The essence here is that if you are part of a decision, you must be the message, not the messenger who distances themselves from decisions. If there are people who disagree with the decision, and they notice that one of the decision-makers does not agree, then it is likely that they will leverage that lack of alignment and sow doubt about the decision. Committing to and being the message is vital.

Another important lens is the power of making decisions in a group versus an individual decision. Daniel Goleman[22] highlights this, "...research has proven the superiority of group decision making over that of even the brightest individual in the group." Tapping into collective wisdom would therefore make for more robust decisions and execution.

👣 Practical steps

Commitment to decisions can be enhanced through an effective decision-making process

- Clarify the problem statement to avoid ambiguity.
- Ensure that assumptions are robustly tested.
- Gather and validate data to support decisions.
- Clarify how decisions will be made.
- Ensure that decisions made can be intuitively explained.

ⓘ Warning signals that a shift is required

- There is general apathy when it comes to making decisions.
- Many meetings are fact-free debates which do not lead to action.
- Many will nod in agreement but disagree afterwards.
- There is a clear lack of commitment to decisions.
- Following up is negatively perceived as micro-management.

📖 Anecdotal business examples

I have observed several times in organisations when there is a lack of commitment to a decision. It often starts in the decision-making process, where there are fact-free debates, apathy towards the process or bystanders who do not actively take part in the decision. They may even say yes, but with no real intention of committing to or ever complying with that decision. I witnessed one example where a leader appeared to agree, but it was evident from his tone and body language that he was not aligned with the decision. He ignored the decision and acted recklessly on a capital project, causing the organisation significant financial damage. What made it worse was that when he was challenged, he believed he was doing the right thing because of his strong opinions. This, despite the agreed decision.

I have also observed the opposite, when organisations have a robust decision-making process and templates. This industrialises decision-making without detracting from the robust dialogue which is essential. In

187

one client, this robust process has enhanced decision-making, resulting in a tangible improvement in bottom-line results. More importantly, the predictability of how leaders become the message has sent clear signals of accountability and responsibility throughout the leadership levels.

> **Business issue for the two stories: Decision-making effectiveness**
>
> *Reminder: As explained in the introduction, the two stories are told as opposite extremes of the mindset transition. Leaders should understand the tensions between the two extremes and find a balance that best fits their context or situation.*

Story 1: Apathy and bystanders

Storm sat back, perplexed by the latest set of results. Following a detailed review, the results did not reflect key decisions made regarding changes to the operating model and the reallocation of team members. He was furious and determined to enforce much-needed discipline amongst his top team. He summoned his assistant and called an urgent management meeting.

As he entered the boardroom, Storm sensed the negative energy. It felt like confirmation of the apathy he had been experiencing from the management team of late. When everyone was seated, Storm lifted the financial report and threw it onto the table. "Can someone please explain why the decisions we agreed on have not been implemented?" There was a stony silence. Storm pointed at the person on his right, "What do you think?"

The executive pushed his chair back slightly. "Well, I was not involved. That makes it difficult to respond."

Storm raised his voice, "You were in the meeting where we made the decision, how can you now pretend to be a bystander?" The executive shrugged without replying. Storm looked around the room, "Anyone else have an excuse?"

One executive moved uncomfortably before replying, "I think the information on which we made the decision may not have been correct. We should never have moved people away from logistics." This brought vigorous nodding of heads, and one after the other, they jumped in, discrediting information and views on which the decisions were made and challenging the results presented in the financial report. One executive also quipped, "I never agreed to losing people in my department." The debate on why the decisions were not made circled for almost two hours, by which time it was obvious that no solution was forthcoming.

Priya, the human resources executive for Brash Inc., paused before trying to leave the room. "I don't know about you, Storm, but these fact-free debates annoy me."

Storm looked up in surprise. "What do you mean by fact-free debates?"

Priya sat down again, "It simply means that people will debate and avoid the real decision or discussion by making random statements or unfounded assertions. They therefore debate with no substantiated facts."

Storm nodded, "Hence the apathy and bystanders. They then become the messengers of the decision, and do not take ownership thereof. They are therefore not the message." Priya nodded in agreement and left the room.

Storm had a restless night as he mulled over possible root causes, and by sunrise, he concluded that the way they made decisions had something to do with it. Arriving at work, he went straight to the finance executive's office. "Hi, Thabo. I've been reflecting on yesterday's meeting. I think that the way we make decisions needs to be overhauled. If we have a better decision-making process, it may be easier to get a commitment from everyone. Please investigate it."

Thabo responded, "I think you're right. It would certainly help in making decisions and hopefully get better commitment. Once they commit to the decisions, hopefully, they will get on with it, and not have us look over their shoulders." Storm nodded and headed for the cappuccino machine.

Thabo examined the best methods and improved how they make decisions. Whilst this improved the decisions and commitments, some results still lagged. During one meeting, Priya asked, "Why do decisions we agree and commit to not translate into timely results?"

After an awkward silence, one of the younger team members whispered, "I don't think we follow through adequately." Several executives looked his way, but it was apparent that nobody else was going to say anything.

Storm paused before concluding, "Well, if we agree at this meeting, you should follow through. I don't think that is my job."

Priya cleared her throat, "Actually, our job is to follow through and provide support. It will improve the commitment to decisions." Reluctantly, Storm nodded.

Story 2: Commitment to decisions

Terry had been reflecting on the latest business results and, over a coffee, had debated possible changes with Thabo, the finance executive. They mulled it over and agreed to call the Executive Team together for a strategic brainstorming session. Thabo asked, "Before we send out the invite, what problem are we solving for?"

The CEO paused before replying, "We need to improve Impact Inc's profitability by looking at the effectiveness of our operating model and deciding whether we should redeploy people and resources to deliver the results we require." Thabo nodded in support. After agreeing, they asked an assistant to convene a strategic brainstorming workshop with the senior leadership team and selected other managers.

Terry welcomed everyone and defined the problem they were seeking to solve. Once he had shared this, he added that this was not about cost reduction, but about reversing declining margins and returning to profitability. Everyone nodded in agreement.

Priya, the human resources executive, kicked off the workshop by sharing important assumptions made in considering the changes to the operating model, including key organisational capability strengths and gaps. One executive raised a hand to challenge one of the assumptions. After some discussion and some amendments, the assumptions were approved.

Next was Thabo, who shared data on headcount and productivity, and informative graphics of how this related to revenue growth and margins. The clarity of the data immediately highlighted potential changes that would improve profitability without limiting the business. Within Impact Inc., decisions that impacted across the organisation were always made with broad consensus, which allowed for speedy decisions, even though some may not agree. The debate was always robust, ensuring the quality of decisions made.

The workshop went very well, and clear decisions were formulated. Terry summarised them in a way that was intuitive and easy to explain. Once he had summarised the decisions, which were captured live on a screen, Terry looked around the room and stated, "In line with our agreed ways of working, even though we may not agree with everything, once we make this collective decision, we are all bound by it." Terry paused for effect before posing a critical question: "Given that we have all had ample opportunity to engage on the information, can I confirm everyone is aligned and committed to the decisions we made today?" Everyone agreed.

Thabo stepped forward and closed the meeting, "Thank you, everyone. I will ensure that the decisions and actions are circulated promptly. This will allow you to take immediate action. Terry and I will provide support and follow up regularly. Finally, a reminder that as a leader in this business, you are the message, not a messenger." A few people chuckled at one of Thabo's favourite expressions.

Terry stayed true to the commitments made and followed up regularly with each member, firstly to provide support, and then to ensure that there was follow-through on key actions emanating from the decisions. Given that following up was an entrenched way of working at Impact Inc., it was accepted as an opportunity to provide feedback, ask questions and seek help.

After a few weeks, Thabo walked into Terry's office with a broad smile, "I've just seen the flash results for the latest month, and I am pleased to say our efforts are starting to materialise. We have shown margin improvements for the second month in a row."

Terry smiled back, "It proves our approach, a commitment to decisions with effective follow-through, delivers results." Terry browsed through the detailed reports and could easily see how their decisions about the operating model had paid off. The robustness of their decision-making process was becoming a competitive advantage.

MINDSET SHIFT 23

Excuses and passing blame ➜ Responsible, accountable and ownership

Question: Do you drive accountability, responsibility and ownership at all levels?

Key mindset transition: Shifting from excuses and passing blame to others to where individuals are given responsibility, are held accountable, and take ownership.

👀 Observations

	Excuses and passing blame	Responsible, accountable and ownership
Expressions (what we hear)	• We cannot tolerate mistakes. • We must find the culprit. • That's a grey area.	• Timely feedback is encouraged. • Robust decision-making debates are accepted. • What are your expectations?
Behaviours (what we see and feel)	• Making excuses is accepted. • Commitments are seldom kept. • Obvious blurring of responsibility and accountability.	• Taking responsibility for one's actions. • Making promises and keeping them. • Ethical integrity is upheld.
Ways of working (what we experience)	• Unrealistic target setting. • Internal fighting. • Blame shifting when things go wrong.	• Space for others to execute. • Question, listen, then act. • Set realistic goals and clear expectations.

🔑 Key message

Responsibility and accountability are frequently used words in leadership, but often the most poorly understood or applied in any organisation. Even in supposedly mature organisations, the confusion created by poor role clarity is oddly pervasive.

In the simplest terms:

- Responsible – when someone is given responsibility or control of a task or project. This is usually given before the task begins.
- Accountable – when someone can be held to account for the success or failure of tasks, actions or decisions. This normally happens during the task, but receives focus when the task is complete.
- Ownership – when someone proactively takes responsibility and accountability and makes the task, project or decision their own. This usually happens throughout the task.

Taking ownership is important for self-motivation and accelerates the execution of work. It contributes to collective organisation efforts, eases ways of working with colleagues and provides a source of personal growth.

Whilst being responsible, being accountable and taking ownership have a lot to do with personal choices of individuals, the leader plays an essential role in creating a conducive environment for this to manifest. As leaders, we enjoy telling people what to do or even doing some of the work ourselves. I classify these as cardinal leadership failures. They reflect an inability to delegate, working at the wrong level and depriving those below you of learning and growth opportunities.

Leaders should be clear about objectives and expectations. They should then ensure that the what and why are understood by team members. Then it is essential to get out of the way and let them get on with the how. If you do not let go, you will create a team that cannot function without you telling them what to do. If a mistake is made, use it as a teachable moment. We have all made mistakes. Our greatest growth and development often come from mistakes.

I also remind you that during your career, someone gave you the why and the what and allowed you to experiment and learn. Hence, why not pay it forward similarly? Besides, they may do it better than you could have.

The most obvious obstacle to this is poorly defined role clarity, often caused by constant changes in organisations, operating models, and the changing nature of work and how it gets done. Poor role clarity creates organisational ineffectiveness, drives blame-shifting and excuses for non-delivery. This is what I term organisational waste. Consequently, role clarity is essential for responsibility, accountability and ownership to thrive.

Two commonly used phrases in role clarity are RACI and RAPID. RACI is more often used for work or tasks, whilst RAPID is more often used in decision-making. These can apply to business processes that involve multiple stakeholders and handover points. When multiple handover points occur, they create an opportunity for confusion, a lack of role clarity or poor decisions. By applying either, a RACI or RAPID, organisational effectiveness is enhanced.

- RACI – responsible, accountable, consulted and informed.
- RAPID – recommend, agree, perform, input and decide.

👣 Practical steps

Key considerations in driving maturity in executing work:

- Overall role clarity in the organisation must be resolved.
- Then, individuals must be given the responsibility to execute.
- They must then be held accountable for the work.
- The next level of maturity is for individuals or teams to take ownership of the work.
- Finally, the individuals or teams can be self-directed, delivering the work without needing to be guided or prompted.

(!) Warning signals that a shift is required

- It is not easy to delegate effectively.
- Excuses prevail when things don't get done.
- When something goes wrong, people are quick to blame others.
- There is a tendency to do it yourself.
- Roles and responsibilities are poorly defined.

Anecdotal business examples

I once facilitated a three-day leadership and strategy workshop in an African country. This organisation had a relatively captive market and was the biggest industry player in that country. Despite this dominant market position, performance and results left plenty to be desired. Executives, the full Board and government representatives all participated in the session. The objective was to find the root cause of the poor financial results. I allowed them to air their thoughts and views for the first morning. I sat there intrigued for four hours, listening to the excuses, blame shifting and even personal insults that were taking place, with everyone wanting to have the last word. Finally, after lunch on the first day, I was given an opportunity to respond. I gave them a hard-hitting lecture on leadership before moving to a broader role clarity discussion for the organisation. Without elaborating on the rest of the three days, it was a reminder of how poor role clarity can be debilitating for organisational performance.

On a personal level, one of the most iconic projects I have worked on was the construction of the Gautrain Rapid Rail system in South Africa. I was one of the eight project directors responsible for the construction of the civil infrastructure for Gautrain. The sheer scale of the project, entailing over ten thousand people spread over an eighty-kilometre construction site, necessitated very rigorous role clarity to achieve on-time project delivery. Whilst we had many people and cultural challenges, the rigour of role clarity and standards was essential for success. It also meant being clear on giving responsibility, managers taking accountability, and everyone taking ownership was critical to success.

Business issue for the two stories: Role clarity

Reminder: As explained in the introduction, the two stories are told as opposite extremes of the mindset transition. Leaders should understand the tensions between the two extremes and find a balance that best fits their context or situation.

Story 1: Excuses and passing blame

Storm was preparing for Brash Inc.'s annual strategy and business planning cycle. He believed he was clear on what Brash Inc. needed to achieve over the next few years. His biggest challenge was ensuring that the leaders of his business units were all aligned with each other, as this synergy was essential for unlocking value and growing earnings and, by implication, the share price. The share price was all-important for Storm, as he had a vested interest through a share option incentive scheme.

Once he had gathered his thoughts, he engaged with Thabo, his finance executive, sharing his thoughts on targets for each business unit and some high-level ideas for changes in the operating model, which he believed would create healthy competition between the business units. He convinced Thabo that his approach would ensure overall growth in the bottom line for Brash Inc. Although Thabo flagged some concerns, Storm was forceful and swayed Thabo to his views.

A few days later, Storm welcomed everyone to the annual strategy and business planning workshop. When everyone was settled, he started, "I have deliberated long and hard on our business planning and what it will take to achieve significant growth in profitability. As you will see on the slide, I have provided each business unit with an annual stretch target of twenty-five per cent for the next five years. I also think it will create a healthy competitiveness amongst you, adding a little spice to our organisation. To achieve this, you will need to be given more autonomy, so I have decided to allow more flexibility in our operating model and the role played by the corporate office in your business. I do not want to bog you down with details of the operating model changes, because you must have more freedom to execute. I hope you are all as excited as I am."

The business unit leaders attempted to probe for specifics related to the targets and autonomy, but Storm deftly skirted the questions and encouraged them to take the opportunity to run their businesses differently. He sensed some resistance, but dismissed it as they probably needed time to digest and internalise his brief.

As the months passed, it became apparent that targets were being missed, and that there were numerous points of contention with the new operating model. Over the past few months, he had ignored objections from Thabo and the business unit leaders on some critical issues, as he genuinely felt that they were making excuses about missing targets. There was a scheduled half-year review, and he was determined to make them understand they were accountable for the targets that had been set.

In kickstarting the half-year review, Thabo presented the business results and analysed business unit results against targets. Only one business unit was tracking on target, whilst more than half had produced lower results than the previous year. He summarised it as a dismal set of results. Storm could feel his frustration and anxiety and called for explanations. He was surprised by the gush of explanations, excuses, and accusations pointing at both the corporate office and the vagaries of the role clarity in the operating model.

Storm was fuming and was about to launch into a tirade at his team when Priya, the human resources executive, called for a break. She smiled at Storm as she headed for a cup of coffee. At first, he was annoyed by the interruption, but something deep down stirred his soul. He realised that the business unit leaders had expressed many deep truths. He caucused with Thabo during the coffee break and was surprised by the frank responses he received. He also had a flash memory of a leadership workshop that dealt with responsibility, accountability and ownership.

When they reconvened, Storm spoke frankly, "I have heard the feedback today, and much as I did not like it, it made me realise that maybe we have made some mistakes. I appreciate that I am accountable for some of the chaos and poor role clarity. Today has been a big lesson for me. I have asked Thabo and Priya to facilitate the next session to explore what we can do differently and what we must change."

Thabo and Priya took over and slowly unpacked the issues and found solutions. Difficult as it was, Storm sat silently, aware of his leadership role in creating the organisation's current status and the lack of results.

Story 2: Responsible, accountable and ownership

Terry was preparing for Impact Inc.'s annual strategy and business planning cycle. Inc. He had a clear view of the strategic direction and the value that could be created for all stakeholders. He also appreciated the challenges in aligning the business units to unlock synergy, including the role clarity changes required for how the corporate office engaged with the business units.

Once he had gathered his thoughts, he engaged with Thabo, his finance executive. He wanted to discuss the business financial targets and clear ideas to refocus the corporate office on the operating model. They engaged robustly and ended the discussion with alignment on strategic direction, financial outcomes, expectations and their message to the business unit leaders.

A few days later, Terry welcomed everyone to the annual strategy and business planning workshop. They started the workshop with a personal check-in, which fostered a human connection between everyone. When everyone was settled, he said, "In preparation for today, we have deliberated on Impact Inc.'s strategic direction, financial outcomes, overall organisational expectations and role clarity. We have set an ambitious target of twenty-five per cent earnings growth for the collective organisation. Whilst this is the outcome and direction, we will collaborate and co-create on how to achieve this. We have also considered previous feedback on the corporate office and will share our thoughts on the business partnering role of the corporate office, as well as improvements in role clarity, which previously hampered execution. I look forward to our collective inputs on how to achieve improved results."

Terry had anticipated some resistance, but when he handed over to Thabo and Priya, his finance and human resources executives, to facilitate the session, he was surprised by the level of frank debate and the ideas which surfaced. When one business leader shared concerns about his challenging market and how a stretch target was near impossible, another stepped in and indicated that with support from others, they could easily unlock opportunities and cover the shortfall. This proved to be a pivotal moment in the workshop, highlighting the value of collaboration and synergy.

Priya then shared her thoughts on changing the roles of business partners from the corporate office. This surfaced a sticky issue related to unrealistic deadlines set by the corporate office. Priya masterfully probed with questions to get to the root cause of the problem. Again, the team rallied around what each person was responsible for and found a speedy solution. Terry closed the workshop, encouraged by the participation, energy and commitment to work together to achieve the results.

As he drove home that evening, he realised that role clarity, accountability and responsibility had been a cornerstone of the successful dialogue.

As the months passed, Terry noted a positive trend in overall results, but the overall result still fell short of the twenty-five per cent target. He had engaged frequently and had a good sense of the issues, and also where they could improve. He was going to share his thoughts at the upcoming half-year review.

In kickstarting the half-year review, Thabo presented the business results and analysed business unit results against targets. Only one business unit was tracking behind target, whilst most business units tracked positively against the prior year, and only one business unit showed no improvement. Thabo thanked everyone for the good financial results. He then invited comments from the business unit. Much to Terry's surprise, each business unit leader stepped up and took ownership of their results. Rather than excuses for missing the overall target, they offered suggestions and solutions for how they might improve results or collaborate more effectively. When the business unit leader with flat growth gave feedback, there was a moment of awkward silence. He said, "I hold myself fully accountable for the lack of growth, and will not use market issues as an excuse. Without support from other business units and the corporate business partners, my results would probably be down by twenty-five per cent. I attribute that improvement to the role clarity we have." This was met with heartfelt applause.

After a lunch break, Terry took it upon himself to facilitate a discussion on how they could continue to improve. He created psychological safety by stating that all ideas would be heard and explored. The balance of the day included robust dialogue, which resulted in concrete actions and delineated responsibility for executing the agreed actions. Terry was satisfied with the day and closed the workshop, "I am utterly convinced that the level of ownership in this business is solid. With this level of commitment, we can only win."

MINDSET SHIFT 24

Mediocrity and complexity ➜ Excellence and simplicity

Question: Does your organisation strive for excellence and simplicity in all they do?

Key mindset transition: Shifting from mediocrity, cultivating complexity and inefficiency, to execution excellence, radical simplicity and effectiveness.

👀 Observations

	Mediocrity and complexity	Excellence and simplicity
Expressions (what we hear)	• Stop complaining and follow the process. • We cannot learn from others. • We're on track, it's just noise.	• What can we learn from others. • Humility/ learning orientation. • Adaptable and knowing there is a simpler way.
Behaviours (what we see and feel)	• Discredit and argue if you have an alternative view. • Listen to what you want to hear. • Lack of feedback skills.	• Encourage effectiveness. • Celebrate improvements and achievements. • Seek out simplicity.
Ways of working (what we experience)	• Policies are a hindrance, and red tape is justified. • No clarity on real value drivers. • Handover points are cumbersome, which cultivates complexity.	• Mistakes used as teachable moments. • Uses sustainable design thinking to solve and eliminate waste. • Resources are optimally used.

🔑 Key message

Driving execution excellence, simplicity and effectiveness requires a systemic view of the organisation, the entire value chain and how these are interrelated. Unlocking value requires a different lens on execution by connecting the dots across multiple handover points using elevated systems thinking. There are two ways of driving execution excellence: the effectiveness of our ways of working, and the efficiency or simplicity of work and processes.

Ways of working refer to how a team works together, collaborates and the rules of engagement. It should lead to connection, belonging, trust, speed, and momentum, all outcomes of collective behaviour and a successful team. Good practises could include collaboration, cross-functional networks and business partnering.

Efficiency in work and processes refers to how efficiently we perform tasks and whether we have optimised processes. Simplicity also implies being intentional about reducing waste. Good practises could include radical simplicity, value chain effectiveness and digitally enabled systems.

As stated, execution excellence is focussed on driving simplicity. In my view, a failure to seek simplicity has the unintended consequence of cultivating complexity. Organisational waste is everywhere and grows over time, cultivating complexity that requires intentional focus to reverse. Examples could include excess motion, multiple hand-offs, excess resources, multiple reviews, resistance to change, manual processing time, searching for the right data, redoing someone else's work, process weaknesses, old processes, waiting time, complexity and poor role clarity.

Value-enhancing activities could include doing different things, doing things differently, reimagining work, redesigning how things are done, applying digital enablers, breaking down silos, leveraging human potential, encouraging creativity and asking open-ended questions.

The absence of focus on execution excellence, radical simplicity and effectiveness will manifest in mediocrity, cultivating complexity and waste. Another tragic observation I have made is that during a crisis or incident, management tends to add more processes or checks and balances, which increases complexity. Seldom do they remove steps, processes or ask what we should stop doing.

Ken Allen in his book Radical Simplicity[23] says, "Execution isn't just about doing the right things – it's about doing them better, faster, more productively and more often than your competitors."

Practical steps

Some considerations for driving execution excellence include

- Adopting a different mindset towards execution excellence.
- Evaluating the effectiveness of ways of working.
- Assessing whether work practices and processes are as effective as possible.
- Being intentional about connecting the dots across the value chain or enterprise system.
- Supporting new approaches to achieving outcomes.

Warning signals that a shift is required

- Execution improvements are addressed in silos.
- The organisation cultivates complexity by only adding to processes and never taking away.
- Obstacles or blockages are well known, but nobody does anything about them.
- Nobody has taken a systemic view of actual work, which limits effectiveness.
- Reducing waste is limited to cost reduction, often only as it relates to headcount.

Anecdotal business examples

A few years ago, I ran a leadership development process for executives and senior leadership of a global multinational organisation. Whilst this gave me intimate insights into the leadership psyche of the organisation, it also gave me a bird's-eye view of how large organisations unintentionally become overly complex. What also struck me was that, by virtue of size, it becomes nearly impossible for organisations to see how they cultivate complexity. I used this phrase deliberately because as large organisations grow, they continually add policies, processes, systems, reporting and rules. Seldom was anyone tasked with taking a step back and reviewing it for simplicity, and even if this happened, the sheer enormity of the task meant that change was unlikely. Whilst this is common in global entities, it is prevalent in almost every organisation I encounter.

On the contrary, I was involved in an organisation with a complex commission structure for sales, which had evolved over many years. It also started to cultivate complexity and drive very siloed and individualistic behaviour. The commission structure and formulas were complex to cater to multiple scenarios. By taking a systemic approach and being clear about what we were solving for, we drove radical simplicity in the formula. It went from many variables to just three. Sometimes we must step away from the complexity to think outside the box.

Business issue for the two stories: Corporate initiatives

Reminder: As explained in the introduction, the two stories are told as opposite extremes of the mindset transition. Leaders should understand the tensions between the two extremes and find a balance that best fits their context or situation.

Story 1: Mediocrity and complexity

Brash Inc. was a local subsidiary of a global multinational organisation based in London. As the local CEO, Storm was responsible for executing both the Brash Inc. strategy and the implementation of core initiatives mandated by the corporate office. Storm was ploughing through the latest instructions from London on the annual strategy process, which included mandated initiatives that he needed to consider and execute . In earlier years, Storm was more willing to comply and find favour with the corporate powers, but recently, these demands had not only drained his energy, but he was becoming increasingly apathetic towards the requirements and excessive complexity.

Knowing full well that his incentives depended on compliance, he would put on a brave face and share the latest expectations and thinking incorporated into Group Initiatives. He dreaded these engagements as he could sense the negativity towards the onerous requirements, and he would often be questioned on why, especially regarding some of the corporate initiatives that had no intuitive linkages to the local context. These initiatives also found their way into KPI's (key performance indicators) without cognisance of the local context.

Storm convened an executive committee meeting to discuss the latest Group Initiatives that had been circulated. He used the presentations to guide his leadership team through the latest expectations. Noticing the dejected expressions on his team's faces, he rallied them, "Hey guys, I know some of these seem to be over the top, but the corporate office would not pursue these if they did not see the value."

Storm braced himself for the normal barrage of responses from his team. They raised them again: lack of understanding from the suits in London, not feasible in our context, not fit-for-purpose, creating complexity, the same resources with increased workload, unrealistic timelines, excessive processes to follow and over-the-top reporting requirements. Storm promised to engage the corporate office again.

During a local visit by a London executive, Storm raised concerns about some initiatives and projects, hoping to get a reprieve on some of them, which, added little value to the ability to execute strategy in the local market. He was met with the normal responses, which were rehearsed because of the frequency of being challenged. Reasons varied, but had common themes, we hired top consultants for new ideas, we need to adopt global best practice, we have to reduce trading risk, we need to show increased compliance, we need to demonstrate best-in-class thinking, our shareholders are demanding greater returns, and the market is watching us closely. Storm sat quietly, aware that he did not buy any of it. The London executive watched closely and said, "As the leader and CEO, you must push your people harder. Next week, we will announce a global headcount reduction of ten per cent. Before you ask, none of the corporate office requirements will change." Storm shrugged his shoulders in timid surrender.

Storm reluctantly started pushing harder for results, but the harder he pressed, the worse the results became. The headcount reductions forced the muscle to be ripped out, and the increased workload on his people caused mental health and burnout challenges. With declining results, London demanded more reporting and enforced greater governance. Sadly, Brash Inc. began losing its best talent, and institutional memory was walking out of the front door, and cuts to management layers created confusion in role clarity.

It wasn't long before the London executive was back, demanding explanations for the declining results, non-conformance to project demands and requests for retention bonuses. He was outspoken, "Storm, your business is a disaster, and your results are not even mediocre, they are a disgrace, given the investment we have made. What do you have to say for yourself?"

Storm sat quietly without responding. His energy to deliver the business had long since evaporated. He also realised in horror that he had not stepped up as a leader and challenged the complexity and excessive demands from London. It dawned on him that he had inadvertently become complicit in cultivating complexity. He looked up at the London executive, his mind scrambling for a sensible response, but nothing was forthcoming.

To his surprise, the executive had also gone quiet, as the realisation of his role in the mediocre results became apparent.

Story 2: Excellence and simplicity

Impact Inc. was a local subsidiary of a global multinational organisation based in London. As the local CEO, Terry was responsible for executing the Impact Inc. strategy and implementation of core initiatives mandated by the corporate office. Terry was reviewing the latest instructions from London on the annual strategy process, which included mandated initiatives that he needed to consider and execute . As he matured as a leader, he was increasingly aware and willing to engage with London on the relevance and applicability of the initiatives cascaded from the corporate office. Terry realised he had a critical role in achieving excellence and driving simplicity across the global group.

Over the years, Terry dreaded sharing the latest corporate initiatives with his Executive Team. Because of deliberate leadership development, he now cherished these engagements. The robust debates about the initiatives were open-minded, and there was a willingness to challenge for relevance and simplicity in execution.

Terry convened an executive committee meeting and joked with his team, "Before I share the latest from London, don't all jump on me and criticise." The team laughed. They were soon attentive and focussed on what was being shared. His Executive Team used the meeting to strengthen their strategic thinking and how they could lead the proposed changes. After a robust debate, many of the initiatives were accepted, but a few were questioned in depth, with alternative suggestions offered which would make them simpler to execute. One initiative was rejected outright, as they felt the complexity created did not justify the effort. Terry agreed and undertook to provide the feedback to London.

During a local visit by a London executive, Terry shared the team's thinking and perspectives on the corporate initiatives with him. The executive responded positively to the feedback and agreed to make adjustments and, in certain cases, exemptions for the local subsidiary. Terry also engaged in the one initiative he felt needed to be rejected, outlining a rational response of the uncertain value added and an intuitive response as to why the complexity and effort were unjustified. The London executive listened carefully, conceded that, with hindsight, it did not make sense, and agreed to stop it. The London executive then sheepishly said, "I think it is only fair to give you an early heads up on a confidential matter. Next week, we will announce a global headcount reduction of ten per cent."

Terry was taken aback, but appreciated the candour and trust placed in him. He replied, "Thank you for the early warning. I expect you will also tell me that no corporate office requirements will change. However, if Impact Inc. is to maintain its results and execution excellence, we must forego some initiatives and obligations to London."

The London executive nodded, "Given that you understand the local context, I am open to ideas. Also, based on your track record, if we can demonstrate profit growth or other savings opportunities, we can be flexible on the headcount reduction." Terry nodded in agreement and thanked him.

Terry waited for the formal announcement, but spent some quality thinking time on how to approach the forthcoming announcement of headcount reduction. When it arrived, he called for his Executive Team to gather. He deliberately shared the exact message from London on the headcount reduction. He paused before continuing, "Having said that, I know this team will think outside of the box, and formulate a response which achieves the outcomes, in a different way. And of course, stating the obvious, protecting our people's jobs." Terry insisted they go away, reflect on the objective and come back with well-thought-through solutions. He did not want any knee-jerk responses.

A few days later, Terry's Executive Team convened a meeting and invited him. They had planned a two-pronged approach to steer the effectiveness of Impact Inc's ways of working and to drive simplicity of work and processes. This was supported by a clear analysis of what really mattered and where they believed the biggest opportunities to eliminate waste would be. The Executive Team shared detailed thoughts on each and asked for Terry's response. He smiled, "Brilliant. I honestly like it. I do have one question. Who will drive this?"

One of his Executive Team spoke up, "We have engaged each other, and agree that we will release two of this team to focus on these efforts for the next six months. It is so critical that we must release the best to make it happen. The rest of us will provide cover for the day-to-day operations."

Terry nodded in agreement. Although he was in awe, he realised that the intentional investment in his team's leadership development was paying handsome dividends. He took comfort that his next engagement with London would be positive and constructive.

PART E

SECOND CAREER

Mindset shift 25: Holding onto success ➔ Life of significance

MINDSET SHIFT 25

Holding onto success ➜ Life of significance

Question: Are you ready to lead a life of significance?

Key mindset transition: Shifting from holding onto success in your career to a life of significance in your retirement years.

👀 Observations

	Holding onto success	Life of significance
Expressions (what we hear)	• Leaving and ending your career badly. • Not knowing when to step down. • Ruling or controlling from retirement.	• Leaving well. • Going out on a high note. • Paying it forward.
Behaviours (what we see and feel)	• Change resistant. • Boastful. • Lack of purpose.	• Gratitude. • Inspirational. • Purposeful.
Ways of working (what we experience)	• Not letting go. • Withholding knowledge and information. • Self-consumed and seeking glory.	• Handing over gracefully. • Coaching and mentoring to pass on knowledge. • Focus on what really matters.

🔑 Key message

In my previous book, *Your Leadership Footprint*, I referred to a plan A, which is your post-corporate role of significance. This is the delicate transition from being a corporate leader to a role of significance and leaving a lasting legacy. This often entails letting go of direct control to a role of influence.

A final role that a leader has in an organisation is knowing when to step down. We have all observed how leaders cling to power, whether as leaders in organisations or political positions. True wisdom and impact can be demonstrated by stepping aside so that the next generation of leaders whom you have nurtured can take over. For many leaders, their leadership roles are often a huge source of energy and purpose and letting go is hard. Obviously, if you are privileged to be in a role where you are fulfilling a greater purpose, and you are still making a significant impact, then please continue. If not, then it is time to move to plan A, where you can make an even greater impact.

However, letting go of something that has been a large part of your life can be a huge disruption, and hard to do. I often hear of senior executives who, after a hectic corporate life, go into retirement with no plans, other than maybe a few rounds of golf and a bit of travel. Sadly, the number of cases of those individuals dying within a few short years is overwhelming. This is largely because they have no purpose after their corporate career.[24]

Creating clarity on your role of significance requires intentional thinking and writing. For many corporate leaders, seeking another role can be challenging because often, work is all they know. Here are a few examples of significant roles:

- Leadership developer.
- Humanity embedder.
- Coach and mentor.
- Growth strategist.
- Solutions thinker.
- Social impact influencer.
- Strategic trends advisor.
- Human potential catalyst.
- Community service provider.
- Educator or teacher.
- Change catalyst.
- Positive influencer.
- Critical thinking advisor.
- Opportunity connector.
- Creator or innovator.
- Win-win partnering advisor.

When you think about it, there are many ways to leave a legacy and pay it forward. Once you have experienced the fulfilment of significance and changing the lives of others, other things tend to feel empty.

👣 Practical steps

Key steps in creating your plan A. Each step requires it to be in writing and constantly refined.

- Deliberate quiet time to reflect on your greater purpose.
- Reflect on your plan "A" career.
- Reflect and test with trusted people in your life.
- Pray until you have peace over it.
- At the right time, put it into action.

ⓘ Warning signals that a shift is required

- You have very little meaning outside of your job.
- You feel that people are pushing you to leave.
- You have little sense of purpose in life.
- You have no idea what life would be like post a corporate career.
- Your family balance is out of sync.

📖 Anecdotal business examples

I will share two examples of actual business leaders, using Storm and Terry as fictional leaders.

Storm had been in the CEO role for fifteen years, and his corporate role was his lifeblood, his source of energy, and pretty much defined who he was. When he considered retirement, it gave him nightmares, especially as he had no other hobbies or ideas of what to do next. This was made worse by colleagues and friends asking him when he was stepping down. He felt like he was being pushed, and this made him progressively crankier and intolerant. The thought of retirement became a mental block and a source of immense frustration. He even started to convince himself that the organisation would fall over the day he left, and without realising the damage he was causing, he was stifling the leadership succession plan. With his retirement date looming, he coerced the Board to award him an advisory consulting contract to support the incoming CEO. At his retirement function, he realised that the incoming CEO was receiving most of the attention, which left him with a hollow feeling. He also overheard someone talking about him, saying, "Storm did not leave well."

214

This angered him, and he was determined to change that as a consultant. Storm had not made the mindset shift from direct control to an influencer. Unwittingly, he still gave instructions and undermined the new CEO. When the Chair called him one day to terminate the advisory consulting arrangement, he was incensed and deeply hurt. This was not how he had dreamt of ending his career. What made it worse was that over the years, he had distanced himself from family and friends, had no post-corporate purpose, and all he could see was a lonely and boring existence.

Terry had been the CEO for eight years and had made a conscious decision not to overstay his tenure as leader. Terry had been successful and thrived as an inspirational leader. He had signalled early that he would be stepping down, and played a proactive role in developing leaders, which gave the Board several strong succession candidates. He became intentional about building capability, transferring knowledge and devolving decision-making to his broader leadership team. He had fulfilled a clear plan from his side, that he could leave well and that there would be no disruption on the day he stepped down. Terry had also heard about plan A from a friend and, over the past two years, he had been building capability and preparing for the time he relinquished the corporate reins. He had been developing a unique leadership development approach and was excited about fulfilling an executive mentoring role for young leadership talent. When he reflected on his new role, he realised it would energise him more than the last year or two as CEO. The leadership transition to the incoming CEO was smooth, and Terry could step back and mentor him to set him up for success. His final month felt like a month-long goodbye with many lunches, thank-you notes and fond farewells. He was offered a position on the Board, which he politely declined. He made it clear that he would always be available for coffee if someone needed a sounding Board. Terry felt good. He was leaving well and had a new purpose, which he could seamlessly switch to. However, he was first looking forward to two weeks in Kruger National Park. After that, he would focus on his plan A. He was energised and raring to go.

This mindset shift does not have stories, as the two anecdotal examples suffice.

Having read the reflective stories throughout this book, what choices will you be making?

BACKGROUND TO THE AUTHORS' LEADERSHIP JOURNEY

When I reflect on my leadership journey and my whole life, I appreciate that I have been truly blessed. Looking back over thirty-five years of working experience, I now value how each experience has been foundational to what is yet to come. I believe that my season to produce fruit is now in my second half.

My school years were underwhelming both academically and in extracurricular activities. I played first team rugby, first team chess, and was selected as a school prefect in my matric year, the latter being the first glimpse of my leadership potential.

My early twenties at university were equally underwhelming, although I held various leadership roles, whether on university house committees or as captain of sports teams. I was frankly clueless about how to lead, but I always had an interest and a desire to lead.

My life changed forever in my mid-twenties when I broke my neck playing rugby and was almost paralysed. My mother's prayers, God's mercy, and my determination to walk again prevailed over my three-year recovery. In my late twenties, it began to dawn on me how fortunate I had been and a wake-up call I needed to live life passionately.

My thirties were more a reflection of how not to lead. Looking back, I realise that my management style was dismal, and I was lucky to get the results I did.

In my mid-thirties, I was privileged to attend Wharton Business School in Philadelphia for a few weeks. The Executive Development Programme I attended was a catalyst for many changes in my life and career. One of the programme directors, Michael Useem, dealt with leadership and signed a book for me with the words, "With best wishes for those leadership moments of your own." This programme led me to leave a CFO corporate role for the first time and venture into management consulting and private equity.

During the early 2000s, I supported the creation of a new mining platform in Murray & Roberts, delisting a mining business, and restructuring the legacy businesses. This required many organisational changes, critical people moments, process development and system changes. I was very blessed to work with Henry Laas, the Managing Director of the platform at the time, and later the CEO of Murray & Roberts. I believe he was the first leader to see my true potential and do something to unlock that potential. This involved working with an executive coach, Godfrey O'Flaherty, who started steering me onto a new people journey.

Being a director on the Gautrain Rapid Rail civils project was another step-change in developing insights into leadership, both from a people's point of view, but also a fundamental crash course in organisational culture. Besides being an iconic project to work on, it proved to be a treasure trove of leadership insights. I fondly remember the project and the mega project employee engagement initiatives I delivered with the HR team.

Post Gautrain, I spent a few more years in the construction industry. During this time, I worked under Luc Jacobs, who was open to exploring leadership, team effectiveness and the value of culture. Together, we experimented and grew. Luc also introduced me to my second executive coach, Elana Godley. Her passion for developing others and finding their potential was life-changing, and it significantly impacted who I was to become. Her most important message was, "Remember to be your authentic self." This message would later manifest powerfully in the leadership development work I do. Bringing myself became the magic sauce in delivering my leadership work.

I returned to management consulting in 2014 and became exposed to the Deloitte CFO Transition Labs early on. I embraced these labs and thoroughly enjoyed facilitating those leadership interventions. This proved to be the next spark on my leadership journey. Over the next few years, I was privileged to run many C-suite leadership interventions and facilitate leadership discussions across the C-Suite, Boards, and senior management teams. Deloitte also allowed me to change careers from finance to human capital and leadership services. During this time, I facilitated leadership sessions with dozens of blue-chip organisations across Africa, Europe and the United States, providing me with rich insights into global leadership trends. It also allowed me to learn from heart-warming stories of many great leaders.

I subsequently joined MAC Consulting to focus on building unique leadership solutions. It was the first time in my career that I had worked for a small business, having always been in large organisations with thousands of employees. Once again, I have been blessed with amazing colleagues, and together we have built incredible leadership and other solutions. My pride and joy is our Exponential Leadership Experience programmes, which have positively impacted hundreds of leaders over recent years.

Over the decade, I have also prayed extensively about my greater purpose in life. God has shown me in countless ways that my purpose is to develop leaders for the future. Whilst I was never destined to become the CEO of a large business, God has equipped me over many years to where I can fulfil my purpose of leadership development and focus on leadership and executive effectiveness. I am encouraged and motivated to know that for each leader I can influence in a positive developmental way, many more people will be indirectly impacted. Living my God-given purpose works for me and ensures I wake up each day ready to make a difference. I could never have imagined this leadership journey, but I would not trade it for anything.

May God steer you on your impactful leadership journey.

ACKNOWLEDGEMENTS

I would like to take this opportunity to thank and show gratitude to those who helped make my latest book a reality.

My wife Esmé and sons Calvin and Bradley for their unwavering support of my writing.

Readers of my previous leadership and fiction novels, who encouraged me to keep writing.

A special thank you to my beta readers: Calvin van der Merwe, Carel Anthonissen, Farren Hester, and Sibusiso Sibisi. Each of you brought unique insights, constructive challenges, and honest feedback. Thank you for your time.

I am blessed with the talent God has given me, allowing me the opportunity to make a difference in the lives of others.

REFERENCES

Allen, K (2019), *Radical Simplicity: How simplicity transformed a loss-making mega brand into a world-class*. London: Penguin Random House.

Bersin, J. (2022). *Irresistible – The Seven Secrets of the World's Most Enduring, Employee-⬛focused Organiszations*. United States. Ideapress Publishing.

Buford, B. (2014). *Drucker & Me: How Peter Drucker and a Texas Entrepreneur Conspired to Change the World*. Franklin, U.S.: Worthy Publishing.

Covey, S.R. (1989). *The 7 Habits of Highly Effective People: Powerful Lessons in Personal Change*. New York: Free Press.

Coyle, D. (2018). *The Culture Code: The Secrets of Highly Successful Groups*. London, UK: Penguin Random House.

Yi, R. (2024). 'Employee Retention Depends on Getting Recognition Right.' Gallup Workplace. Retrieved from: https://www.gallup.com/workplace/650174/employee-retention-depends-getting-recognition-right.aspx

Goleman, D, Boyatzis, R & Mckee. A. (2002). *The New Leaders: Transforming the art of leadership into the science of results*. London: Sphere.

Heskett, J. L., & Hallowell, R. (1993). Southwest Airlines (A & B). Harvard Business School Case Study 9-694-023.

International Association of Oil & Gas Producers (OGP). (2014). *Safety Culture in the Oil and Gas Industry: Guidance for Developing a Safety Culture Program*. OGP Report No. 452.

Maxwell, J. C. (n.d.). 'The single biggest way to impact an organization is to focus on leadership development.' [Quotation]. Retrieved from: https://quotefancy.com/quote/841029/John-C-Maxwell-The-single-biggest-way-to-impact-an-organization-is-to-focus-on-leadership

Schmidt, E., Rosenberg, J. & Eagle, A. (2019). *Trillion Dollar Coach: Leadership Handbook of Silicon Valley's Bill Campbell*. London: John Murray Publishers.

Seligman, M. (n.d.). ⬛"*The aim of positive psychology is to catalyse a change in psychology from a preoccupation only ⬛with repairing the worst things in life to also building the best qualities in life.*" [Quotation]. Retrieved from: www.azquotes.com/author/20352-Martin_Seligman

Sinek, S. (2009). *Start with Why: How Great Leaders Inspire Everyone to Take Action*. New York: Penguin Books.

Zander, R.S., & Zander, B. (2002). *The Art of Possibility: Transforming Professional and ⬛Personal Life*. New York: Penguin Books, 2000.

Zenger, J.H. & Folkman J.R. (2009). *The Extraordinary Leader: Turning Good Managers into Great Leaders*. New York: McGraw Hill.

Van der Merwe, D. (2022). *Your Leadership Footprint: How will you be remembered?* Bryanston, Johannesburg: KR Publishing.

ENDNOTES

1   Maxwell, n.d.

2   Seligman, n.d.

3   Buford, 2014.

4   Maxwell, n.d.

5   Buford, 2014.

6   Goleman, Boyatzis & Mckee, 2002.

7   Coyle, 2018.

8   Yi, 2024.

9   Covey, 1989.

10 van der Merwe, 2022.

11 Schmidt, Rosenberg & Eagle, 2019.

12 Sinek, 2009.

13 Zenger & Folkman 2009.

14 Zander & Zander, 2002.

15 Zenger & Folkman 2009.

16 Schmidt, Rosenberg & Eagle, 2019.

17 Schmidt, Rosenberg & Eagle, 2019.

18 Goleman, Boyatzis & Mckee, 2002.

19 Bersin, 2022.

20 International Association of Oil & Gas Producers (OGP),

21 Heskett & Hallowell, 1993.

22 Goleman, Boyatzis & Mckee, 2002.

23 Allen, 2019.

24 van der Merwe, 2022.

INDEX

www.ingramcontent.com/pod-product-compliance
Lightning Source LLC
Chambersburg PA
CBHW051209200326
41519CB00025B/7055